THE COMPLETE BOOK OF PITFALLS

THE COMPLETE BOOK OF PITFALLS

A Victim's Guide to Repairs, Maintenance, and Repairing the Maintenance

DERECK WILLIAMSON

With drawings by the author

Galahad Books • New York City

Portions of this book appeared in slightly different form in "Phoenix Nest" in *The Saturday Review*.

Copyright © 1971 by Dereck Williamson

All rights reserved. No part of this work may be reproduced or transmitted in any form or by any means, electonic or mechanical, including photocopy, recording, or any information storage and retrieval system, without permission in writing from the publisher.

Library of Congress Catalog Card Number: 73-82286

ISBN 0-88365-058-4

Published by arrangement with the McCall Publishing Company

PRINTED IN THE UNITED STATES OF AMERICA

Design by Tere LoPrete

"Why do they call it Beaverboard? Is it because beavers eat it, or because beavers don't eat it?"
—Jack Prescott

Contents

Introduction	3
I. Unselected Risks and Other Assorted Perils	
POWER FAILURES	13
TELEPHONE FAILURES	15
EARTH-SINKING	15
THE STEALTHY VINE	16
THE HUMIDITY PROBLEM	17
BATS IN THE ATTIC	19
MEN WITH MASKS	20
ISOLATION	20
THE SOCIAL TERMITE	21
GYPSY MOTHS	24
II. Maintenance, Repairs, and Repairing the Maintenance	
TOOLS	31
GLUE TIME	37
PLUMBING AND HEATING	41
REPAIRING TOILETS	45
APPLIANCES	48
ELECTRICAL WORK	56

Contents

HOUSE PAINTING	60
INTERIOR PAINTING	64
SPRAY PAINTING	68
WALL COVERING	70
SCREENS AND STORM WINDOWS	75
A WEEKLY GARBAGE SCHEDULE	79
SHEET METAL WORK	82
WHEN YOUR MAILBOX FLUNKS	83
PREVENTIVE MAINTENANCE	85

III. *Home Improvement and Rainy-Year Projects*

A COTTON-PICKING HOBBY	93
CONCRETE	95
ROOM DIVIDERS	98
NEVER A NULL MOMENT WITH A SHARP BROAD ADJUSTMENT	102
THE MOVING PLASTIC WRITES . . .	107
WHAT GOES UP MUST FALL DOWN	109
BUILD AN ASHTRAY	110
LANDSCAPING AND GARDENING	113
WHILE-YOU'RE-AT-IT PROJECTS	118
TREE HOUSES	122
HOUSEBUILDING DON'TS	123

IV. *Timely Tips for Tipply Times*

BEE PREPARED	129
WHAT'S THE POINT?	130
COLLECTING COAT HANGERS	130
PIGS AT SPEED	131
DOWN WITH WATTAGE	132

Contents

STORING SMALL PARTS	132
SCREWING UP A CHAIR	132
FETCHING WRONG WRENCHES	133
TOTEM POLES AT HOME	133
NAILING BOARDS	134
DIVIDING BOARDS	134
FASTENING THINGS TO WALLS	134
OPENING OTHER GARAGES	135
PARKING TIP	136
PARKING TRICK	137
BASHING A PORCH	137
WATER AND OIL	137
WEARING OUT FROM NO WEAR	137
ONE LEG OUT	138
HEATING UP BIRDS	138
CHOKING ROSES	138
SPACE-SAVER	139
LEAVE FOLDING CHAIRS ALONE	139
INSTALL VALVES	139
FUNNY-SOUNDING PIPES	139
POINT TO PONDER	140
SHADY PAINTING	140
UNLEVEL LEVELS	141
DOGS KNOW THESE THINGS	141
TIME TIP	142
THE TREE RACE	142
INSTANT BAD FURNITURE	143
HAVE AN ORNAMENT SHOOT	143
THE SPORTING LIFE	143
LOOK-ALIKE HAZARDS	143

Contents

MATTRESSES RESIST	144
HOW TO BE QUOTED	145
"HANDYMAN'S SPECIAL"	146
FLOOD-IT-YOURSELF	146
RELOCATION GUIDELINES	147

THE COMPLETE BOOK OF PITFALLS

Introduction

For a long time—at least since last Thursday—the public has awaited a sensible, no-holds-barred, manual on home projects and repairs. The would-be handyman is weary of reading about "easy weekend projects" which take several years to complete, like digging a cellar under the house or adding a second floor. He wants to be told the truth for a change. And he wants to know what can go wrong. Instinct tells him that to accomplish the aforementioned projects, there will be a lot more to Step One than just "Jack Up House," or "Remove Roof and Temporarily Set Aside."

The do-it-yourselfer is tired of seeing pictures of happy couples in evening clothes stapling insulation between the rafters. Few marriages can survive a complete attic conversion. Have you ever tried to install a new ceiling with the help of loved ones? Did anyone stay clean? Calm? Was anybody smiling? Can you straighten out your neck yet? How many months has it been that way now?

Impractical information is just as bad as incomplete information. The handyman is fed up with those monthly magazines like *Everyday Mechanics* and *Popular Technology* which tell you how to make things from bizarre parts.

Introduction

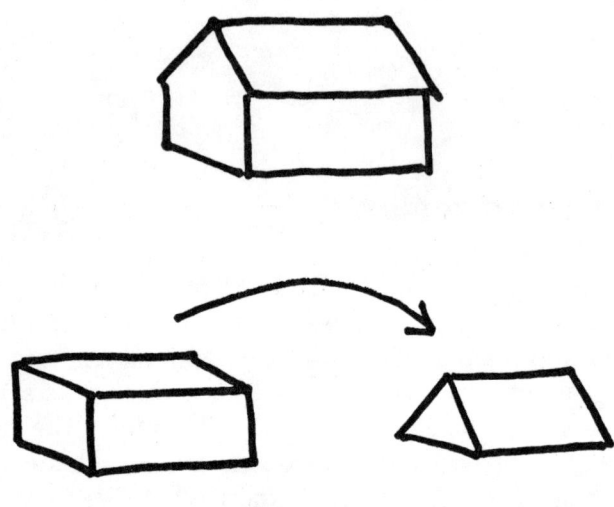

Step One

Don't toss out those Sherman tank thrust bearings! Weld them on the ends of 1936 Oakland camshafts wrapped with 5,000 feet of old transatlantic cable stripped of insulation. Bolt on two old seventy-five-pound mushroom anchors, and you have a couple of fine revolving outdoor patio lamp-post barbecue grills!

The same publications give generous space to boastful letters detailing improbable projects no sane person would think of undertaking.

My wife was always complaining about her clothesline sagging under a full load of wash. I solved the problem by attaching a six-inch drum spindle to my lathe and turning out a hexagonal

Introduction

spline, chamfered at one end to take a modified .0019-inch stove bolt. Then I brazed a plastic C-clamp to the other end, and padded the entire assembly with the felts from an old player piano. Now, by simply inserting six cotter-pins in the plate facing, the spliced spring-slung spindle spline shims take up the clothesline slack in a jiffy. In colder weather, of course, a thermocoupler must be used. I picked up mine in a Russian junkyard for only a few kopecks.

And finally, there are all those impossible solutions to common problems.

If your shower suddenly runs out of hot water and the ice-cold water makes you faint, try replacing the shower stall. If that doesn't help, look to see if mineral deposits are being shuffled off the mortal coil. If so, resolder the connections in high places. Then reset the points, being careful not to disturb the magneto and timer. The shower will give you no further trouble.

This book cuts through all that nonsense and deals in a practical manner with familiar home subjects like repairs, maintenance, and repairing the maintenance. It avoids way-out home-improvement ideas—"Put a Patio Around Your Septic Tank!", "Use Your Chimney as a Laundry Chute!"—which give building and health inspectors writer's cramp and reduce the value of your home to zero. Also conspicuously absent in this book is the list of new products nobody ever heard of. It's time the

Introduction

truth was told. You'll never find the new plastic metallic concrete resin at your local drugstore; the home-improvement columnists are just putting you on.

The following chapters tell it like it really is. You'll learn what happens when concrete forms collapse. You'll find out why it's not such a hot idea to divide a room with too many room dividers. You'll meet the social termite. You'll learn how to get the little black slice of diet bread out of the toaster. You'll see the wisdom of not wearing a necktie while wallpapering. And you'll discover many of the pitfalls of home ownership. Falling into pits is one of them.

For those who don't have the right tools for jobs around the house and apartment, there's a special chapter on using the wrong tools. There's a section on unselected risks, which tells you what happens if you don't watch out, and what happens if you do watch out. (The same thing happens, either way.)

Do-it-yourself projects save money, as long as you don't have to redo-it-yourself or get professional assistance, known locally as "calling for help." Many people get involved in home projects for other than financial reasons. For one thing, it's an excellent escape route. A man who doesn't know his T-joint from his elbow will cheerfully tackle a complex plumbing job when faced with the alternative of attending a child's four-hour dance recital. ("I just can't make it, Honey; that pipe'll go any time and flood out all your nice furniture and drapes. God knows how I'll manage with no plumbing experience, but I've got to give it the old college try!")

If you lack the courage to undertake a job you think is over your head, write it down on a Special Project list. One Sunday afternoon you'll glance out the window

Introduction

and spot that surprise carload of relatives. Set Condition Crud. Quickly remove specially prepared greasy coveralls from their plastic bag. While slipping them on, glance at your list and choose a project. Dive down the cellarway like a rat. By the time Aunt Fran and Uncle Fran and their seven kids get inside the house, you should have half the furnace taken apart. They'll all stay away from you because you're dirty. You can counter any attempts at conversation with muttered curses, ostensibly directed at a stuck damper. Finally they'll go upstairs and leave you alone. And you'll stay on the job because there's no place else to go. Later, when they've all left, you'll be able to emerge from the cellar with the proud knowledge that you've been simultaneously fixing a furnace and foxing a family. Now all you've got to do is get the new parts, and put the furnace back together again. Keep at the job, and you'll have heat almost before the first frost.

This book describes many interesting escape projects in detail. One of them will take you the bad part of a year. None can be done over a weekend. There is no such thing as a "weekend project." The only thing you can accomplish in one weekend is go away for it.

I

UNSELECTED RISKS AND OTHER ASSORTED PERILS

If you want to cheer yourself down, take a good look at the section in your homeowner policy titled "Perils Insured Against." You'll discover that you've got more than a dozen perils coming to you, including:

"Removal, meaning loss or removal of the property covered hereunder from premises endangered by the perils insured against."

That doesn't make much sense, does it? But it sure is scary. Read it several times. It begins to sound like the entire property might be removed, say while the family is out roller skating. But it doesn't mean that. What they're talking about in their own meaningless way is removing things from the house in time of peril. If you damage the sofa while tossing it out the picture window during an earthquake, you're covered. Just for the sofa, though.

You are also insured against "Sudden and accidental tearing asunder, cracking, burning, or bulging of a steam or hot water heating system." Another listed peril is the "Sudden and accidental tearing asunder, cracking, burning, or bulging of appliance for heating water for domestic consumption." It's enough to make a man move his whole family out into the garage.

Collapse of the house itself is listed as a peril. So is (1) Fire, (2) Aircraft, (3) Falling Objects. Number 3 is evidently some sort of Chicken Little Clause, since Aircraft is already covered in Number 2.

The fine print lists certain "Special Exclusions." These take the company off the hook for losses "caused by, resulting from, contributed to or aggravated by any mud flow." That's a bad clause, as anybody with small children will tell you.

The truth is, insurance policies are hopelessly inadequate. Things in the house rarely bulge or tear asunder. That happens outside. (See chapter on pouring concrete.) The most common perils aren't even listed as special exclusions. Every day, people encounter home emergencies that neither they nor insurance underwriters ever dreamed of. Some of these crises may seem like small ones, but they get to you. You'll collapse long before the house does.

There are plenty of articles, books, and pamphlets dealing with common catastrophes such as landslides ("What to Do When Boulders Pass Through Your Home"); hurricanes ("When Windows Drop In Unexpectedly"); floods ("Small Boat Handling in Your Cellar"); and tornadoes ("If Your House Should Fall on a Wicked Witch"). But most people already know what to do in those emergencies—crawl under a strong table and tune the radio to an emergency-broadcast beeeeeeeeeeeeeeeep. The ear-splitting tone gives you a migraine and takes your mind off the catastrophe.

Ordinary-headache domestic hazards receive little attention in print, unfortunately. Few people know what to do when a mailbox springs a leak and soaks everything addressed to "Occupant." And how does one un-freeze a cellar water pipe?

The answer to the first problem is to buy a smaller

Unselected Risks and Other Assorted Perils

mailbox and put it inside the leaking one. To thaw a water pipe, take apart the clothes dryer pipe and redirect the hot air.

Note carefully that in neither case have you really solved the problem. But you've *coped* with it. And that's the secret of handling the following assortment of unselected risks.

Power Failures

Power rarely fails in large cities. When it does, most people know what to do—steal candles from the nearest church, mug senior citizens, get pregnant. Be on the lookout for newspaper reporters who will want to know where you were when the lights went out, and what you thought it was at first. If, for some peculiar reason, you have a flashlight in your apartment and that flashlight has batteries in it, just sit tight. The word will get around and you'll be interviewed on the radio the next day. If you have a portable camp stove and lanterns, television stations will battle for the privilege of filming your life story.

In the country, though, power failures are so common that rural weeklies mention them only in roundup stories ("Last Week's Blackouts"). The explanation is simple. Power lines are strung along country roads under tree limbs. Each winter, to the amazement of power company officials, ice forms on the trees, the limbs snap, and the wires are torn down. Trained crews rush out to put them back again, often skidding off the road and knocking down their own poles. While all this is going on, your home will be without electricity.

The Complete Book of Pitfalls

Be prepared. Get in shape for the emergency. Do wrist exercises so you can operate old-fashioned can openers. Practice not looking at TV. Toughen your body to withstand cold. Decrease your electric blanket settings until you can survive for several hours with the current off. Finally, sleep on the garage floor wrapped in leaves.

Anticipate power failures by watching for ice forming on trees. Sitting at the kitchen table drinking coffee and watching ice build up on trees is a lot more interesting than working around the house.

If you think the power might fail at any moment, take swift steps. Rural people know that the first thing to do is fill the bathtub with water. It is comforting to have a bathtub full of water. After the emergency is over, you let the water out.

If a child is already in the tub when you want to fill it, be patient. You mustn't panic him. Tell him to get out of the tub. The child may argue that his bath is not finished. Explain to him that you wish to fill the tub with water. The child may argue that the tub is already full of water. Explain to him that if the electricity goes off, so will the pump that draws the water from the well. Make him understand that the family needs a supply of drinking water, and that the tub is presently full of soap and plastic ducks and wooden tugboats. The child may respond by tossing out all the toys and taking a healthy swallow of his bath-water. "See, I can drink it!" Be firm. Get him out of there.

Before a power failure, put the cat in a safe place. Otherwise she may fall down the stairs. The ability of a cat to see in the dark is highly overrated.

If you have matches, candles, a bottle-gas or kerosene stove, flashlights, extra batteries, and a genuine enthu-

Unselected Risks and Other Assorted Perils

siasm for boredom you will be able to weather a short power failure quite comfortably. If the power stays off for any length of time, it's nice to have a fireplace or a heating stove. Wearing five coats in the house all winter makes you round-shouldered.

Telephone Failures

Telephones play an important role in everyone's life. Malfunctioning instruments and inadequate networks keep you in a constant rage, good for healthy blood circulation. As an outlet for pent-up emotions, you can't beat screaming into a telephone. Telephones benefit shut-ins who, when lonely, can dial almost any combination of numbers and get a recording.

When telephone wires are torn down in a storm it's not as serious as downed power lines, however. That's because when there's a telephone breakdown, most people don't know the difference.

Failure of the telephones to work in recent years is credited with bringing people closer together. Time and again, a person has visited the house or apartment of a stranger to report an out-of-order phone, only to find that the neighbor's phone isn't working either. Soon others arrive. Finally everybody gives up, gathers round the table, and breaks bread.

Earth-Sinking

Earth-sinking, like mud flow, is usually excluded from insurance policies. The most common form of earth-sinking is around a freshly graded foundation where you've planted expensive ornamental shrubs. Ever so slowly, the little bushes will sink out of sight. Soon there will be a trench around the house, and it will fill up with beer cans. A yew or juniper in a trench surrounded with beer cans doesn't get enough sunlight.

Wait until the ground next to the foundation settles before planting anything there. Settling sometimes takes several years. If you're lucky, you'll be transferred again before you have to do any foundation planting.

Another kind of earth-sinking happens after you dig a big hole in the front lawn and later fill up the hole using the same dirt. (There are all sorts of reasons for digging a big hole in the front lawn. For instance, many people like to examine their tree roots now and then, to see how they're getting on.) When you put the dirt back in the hole, it won't all fit in there. It will make a mound. Tell people that Chief Leaping Limping is buried there. Gradually, the dirt will settle to lawn level. But then it will keep on settling until you have a little hollow to collect stagnant water and breed mosquitoes.

No matter how many times you add dirt to level off the hollow, it will sink down again. This is the Law of Diminishing Dirt. After a while, you'll give up and plant flowers in the hollow.

The Stealthy Vine

The problem of an outside plant going inside is common to quaint old stone houses held together with ivy. One day you will discover a little vine sneaking along the top of the bookshelf, unusual because there is no house plant on the bookshelf.

Unselected Risks and Other Assorted Perils

Take a deep breath. Examine the vine. Follow it along the wall. See where it comes through the crack between the stones. Go outside. See where it goes in through the crack between the stones.

Do not cut the vine off. If you do, two more vines will enter the house. Then four; then eight. Don't get a vine mad. Cooperate with it by stringing wire around the room. The vine will follow it, and it will get longer and longer.

Sometimes late at night you will be able to hear it, growing.

The Humidity Problem

When your doors shrink down until they look like old-fashioned saloon doors, or when they swell so it takes an ax to get them open, chances are you've got a humidity problem. Although humidity problems can be cured temporarily by carpentry—adding and subtracting little pieces of wood throughout the house as the seasons change—it is wiser to seek a permanent solution. Regulating the humidity is the answer.

Most homes are either too dry or too damp. How can you determine the condition of your own house? First of all, avoid technical pamphlets that get you all involved in "relative humidity," a term that makes just about as much sense as "degree days." (Relative humidity is getting steamed up when your loudmouth cousins from Teaneck show up.) A simple checklist can be used to pinpoint humidity troubles.

The house is too damp if:
1. Shoes in the closet all turn green.

The Complete Book of Pitfalls

2. Drop-leaf table leaves, which normally hang straight down, curl upward as if preparing for flight.

3. The walls take on a greenish tint.

4. Cattails start growing in the corner of the living room, and mushrooms sprout in the linen closet.

5. More than the usual number of herons and flamingos congregate in the kitchen.

6. All the rooms grow green wall-to-wall carpeting.

7. Green fuzz begins to appear all over your body.

The house is too dry if:

1. Furniture starts coming apart at the joints.

2. You must communicate with others by clutching your throat and uttering a series of croaks.

3. The walls crack.

4. You can't walk barefoot on rugs because of the young cacti.

5. Your clothes cling to you, your hair stands up, and every time you reach for a metal object a spark gives you a shock.

6. While crawling out to the kitchen at night for a drink of water, you see a mirage.

7. Little pieces of your skin begin falling off.

To solve a dampness problem, you need a dehumidifier. For dryness, a humidifier is the answer. Don't order the wrong one; you'll compound the problem. Portable humidifiers and dehumidifiers are popular; they're about the size of television sets, only the picture isn't so hot. You plug them in, and they go to work taking moisture out of the air or putting it in, as the case may be.

Wealthy sportsmen often buy one of each, put them in a room face to face, switch them on, and take bets. But the average homeowner doesn't want to play around with humidity. He's just interested in saving his own skin and/or keeping it from turning green.

Unselected Risks and Other Assorted Perils

Bats in the Attic

The adage "If you think you've got mice, you've got 'em" doesn't apply to bats. With bats, you know. Nothing else flies like that (a bat flies like a wounded bat), or hangs from the rafters looking like a wounded bat hanging from the rafters.

When you discover a bat in your attic, don't jump out the window. Remember, bats won't hurt you, according to the experts. In the next breath the experts say that you shouldn't pick up a "sluggish" bat because it may have rabies and bite you. They don't bother to explain the difference between a sluggish bat and one who's just goofing off, a slugabed bat. Experts are like that. They also tell you that vampire bats live only in South and Central America. But suppose that thing hanging up there is *visiting*?

A calm retreat is the best policy. Remember, a bat won't get caught in your hair unless—but there's no sense going into all that now. Pretend to ignore the bat and casually stroll back to the attic hatchway. Then gracefully leap through to the floor below, slamming the trapdoor behind you.

Bat literature is available complete with dissertations on the social habits of the creatures: what they eat, where they go, who they see. Nobody wants to read that stuff. So bats eat insects, big deal. Take a real close look at a bat sometime. You'll vote for the insects.

The solution to bats in the attic is a simple one. Keep the attic closed at all times. Don't go up there. Bats have their territory; you have yours.

Men with Masks

In rural areas when the winter snow lies deep, men with masks will come to the house. The masks are made of black wool, and cover the entire face. Holes for eyes, nose, and mouth are hideously trimmed in red wool.

The housewife may be startled, especially if she is alone and isn't expecting masked men. But there is nothing to worry about.

The men are members of the snow-plowing crew whose truck has broken down. They'll want to use the telephone. Sometimes they can be persuaded to take off their masks and have coffee.

Isolation

Women who move to the country quickly realize that the most immediate emergency, the most common peril, is isolation. There is no next-door neighbor to talk to. There is no next door, just woods filled with animals that crash and stumble through the leaves. If you were brought up on nature stories about sure-footed beasts silently gliding through the forest, it comes as a shock to learn that real rabbits and squirrels spend their spare time jumping up and down on dry twigs.

You must learn to live with sudden noises. After a while you won't be leaping out of your chair as much. In the summer you'll go through the whole thing all over again with frogs bellowing from the pond all night.

Another peril is forgetting how to talk. With only pre-

Unselected Risks and Other Assorted Perils

schoolers to converse with all day, you'll develop careless speech habits. When you eventually leave the house for a rare social gathering, such as the Plumber's Ball, you'll find yourself greeting your hostess:

"How do you do? On the way here, guess what I saw? Can you guess? It was a pretty birdie, way way high up in a tree. Can you guess what color the birdie was? It was orange. It was an oriole. Oriole. Can you say oriole? Don't just stand there with your mouth open. You can say oriole. Say it! You know perfectly well that you can say oriole. You're just being stubborn. You must be tired. It's time for your nap."

When you find yourself slipping into short sentences, take immediate action. Practice talking at home. Turn on the radio and argue with the announcer. Go outdoors and deliver noise-abatement lectures to the animals. Read your insurance policy aloud. Do anything to keep your mind from sudden and accidental tearing asunder, cracking, burning, or bulging.

Watch for Signs of Termites

The Social Termite

Termite pamphlets read like sociology textbooks, and it is small comfort when your house is collapsing to learn that:

"Termites are social insects that live in nests and col-

The Complete Book of Pitfalls

onies within foundation walls and adjacent soil areas. The colony is composed of three forms or castes—swarmers, workers, and soldiers."

One can readily envision this proud race, cultural patterns unchanged for centuries, living an idyllic life in a cozy colony. In one part of the village the swarmers are getting ready for the 1:30 P.M. flight, and there is the excited chatter and bustle of last-minute packing. Most of the soldiers are in the mess hall, wisecracking their way through the noon meal of creamed chipped beef on oak. The remaining soldiers are relaxing at their guard posts, chewing toothpicks and watching the chanting workers coming through the gate with parts of your garage.

A termite pamphlet is not something you would normally have lying around the house, nor do you pick it up at the library for light summer reading. You got the termite pamphlet from the agricultural agent because the other day you were scraping paint near the foundation, and the scraper plunged into the corner-post and you dug around and discovered the post was hollow. And you poked around some more and dug out lots of squirming little white things ugh yuk.

Now you are reading the pamphlet for two reasons: to find out if those little white things are termites, and to get advice on how to kill them. It's discouraging to come upon passages like "The worker builds delicate little brown mud tubes and works busily night and day to keep his colony supplied with food in the form of cellulose."

You turn to a diagram showing a worker termite, a flying ant, and a flying termite. The pamphlet elaborates: "The sudden appearance on a spring day of a swarm

Unselected Risks and Other Assorted Perils

of winged termites inside the house is the most common indication of a termite colony. The insects should be carefully compared with the illustration to determine whether they are ants or termites. Termites that have dropped their wings can be distinguished from ordinary ants by the absence of a 'wasp waist.' Both ants and termites may exist in the same building, and each group may produce a swarm at various times during the year. Therefore it is necessary to examine each swarm closely to determine if termites or just the relatively unimportant winged ants are present."

Faced with the prospect of measuring termite and ant waists with a little tape measure, many homeowners wisely call in an exterminator.

If you've never been visited by an exterminator, you're in for a surprise. Although exterminating is a serious business, the exterminators themselves are a bundle of laughs. They normally bring two trucks, so they can race each other on the way over. They skid into your driveway with horns beeping. Grinning and shouting and waving, they bounce from their trucks and start to haul out hoses and pumps and drums and drills.

The leader examines the bad post. "Ho ho, you got carpenter ants!"

You show him the pamphlet and point to the picture of the worker termite, ". . . a cream-colored, blind, soft-bodied insect that cannot withstand the drying effect of exposure to the air."

"Right, man. You got them, too!" the leader exclaims, doing a little dance step and ripping off a long board. Two of his helpers, hysterical with laughter, are spraying each other with portable insecticide pumps. A fourth man has plugged in a huge drill and is boring holes in your concrete garage apron. Every time he finishes a hole he giggles.

At this point it is prudent to retreat into your house. The frequent outbursts will keep you posted on what's going on out there. And the leader will report directly whenever he finds something really funny, like tunnels of the powderpost beetle.

By the time the men have finished, packed up, and roared off delirious from joy and insecticide, the whole community will know you've got bugs. Neighbors, relatives, friends, and enemies all will have driven by slowly to look at the white trucks with EXTERMINATOR lettered on the sides.

Soon your home will be known locally as "The Termite House." If you think that's quaint, wait until you try to sell it.

Gypsy Moths

If you haven't ordered any bulldozer work and you notice one day that all your trees are gone, chances are you have a gypsy moth problem. What you actually have is a gypsy moth caterpillar problem, if that makes you feel any better. The caterpillars are the larvae of the gypsy moth and they've got to eat your trees to gain strength to turn into moths so they can eat other things. Maybe your clothes.

The United States Department of Agriculture conducts annual air strikes against gypsy moths, penetrating deep behind their lines with chemical spray. Experts say that the program is necessary because the caterpillars eat holes in tree leaves. After each spraying, holes are

Unselected Risks and Other Assorted Perils

observed in tree leaves. One popular theory is that although the spray kills the insects it has a bad side effect; it eats holes in tree leaves. That's probably just rumor, but it does have the ring of a federal program.

Gypsy moth defoliation isn't the only bad thing that can happen to your trees, of course. There are all sorts of fascinating tree diseases, including one called shoestring root-rot. When you climb into your hammock the two trees slowly come together and you sink to the ground.

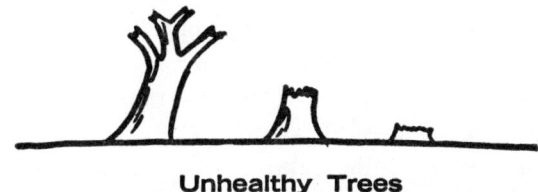
Unhealthy Trees

When you see a tree losing its leaves, phone the Department of Agriculture and they'll send over a World War I Spad to spray your gypsy moths and your children. Don't turn in a false alarm, though. First make sure that insects are responsible for the leaf loss. There is a certain time of year when the leaves are *supposed* to fall off the trees.

Spray areas are determined by surveys. This summer you may be visited by a moth survey man who will ask your permission to place little paper cups containing "a sex attractant" on your property. These fellows have a rough job; women are always hitting them with brooms.

The paper-cup traps are tacked to tree branches. Each cup has a lid with a small hole in the center. It is difficult to see how a moth, even one burning with lust, could climb inside the cup without considerable effort, twisting and turning this way and that. But that's what makes it all worthwhile, eh, gypsy moth?

The moth survey men mark the location of their sex-in-a-cup stations with bright orange pennants. Additional pennants are fastened at the edge of your property, usually on roadside stakes. These little flags attract quite a bit of local attention: church groups and the local decency league raise a ruckus. You may even be accused of operating a mothel. But the harassment won't last. After about a month of hanky-panky in the woods, the Department of Agriculture will gather up all the traps and take them back to the laboratory for a "study" behind closed doors. Results of the survey are then turned over to the military-agricultural complex which selects spraying targets for the following year.

As might be expected, the spray program is highly controversial. Each year thousands of nasty letters are fired off to newspapers, congressmen, the Department of Agriculture, and the Spad people. Many conservationists feel that the cute little gypsy moths with their tiny red bandannas and golden earrings are in danger of extinction unless they are protected, and taught not to steal trees.

(Gypsy moth spray also kills bees. If you keep bees you'll have to go out and put a little gas mask on each one just before the plane comes over.)

Additional weapons in the antimoth arsenal are a wilt disease which shrinks the caravan, and a bacterial spray which breaks down the gypsy moth's system and stampedes his horses.

Recently, the agriculture brains have been talking about importing parasitic flies and "tiny wasps" to prey

Unselected Risks and Other Assorted Perils

on gypsy moths. Presumably, the flies and wasps could later be eliminated by specially imported miniature rattlesnakes, dwarf scorpions, and midget black widow spiders.

In the meantime, if you hear the faint sound of guitars and discover little wagon-ruts in your flowerbed, you know you've got gypsy moths. Don't make any deals with them for a new roof or driveway, and don't believe what they tell you about materials left over from another job. Hold on to your wallet and wait for the government spray plane. Perhaps this time it will be a Sopwith Camel.

II

MAINTENANCE, REPAIRS, AND REPAIRING THE MAINTENANCE

Tools

They say it's important to use the right tool for the right job, but actually it's not all that important. The wrong tool can be used for the right job, and it is often handier. A silver grapefruit spoon makes a good wrong screwdriver, for example. You can usually bend it back into shape afterward.

The tools required most often for jobs around the house are a screwdriver, a hammer, and a pair of slip-joint pliers. They are kept in a kitchen drawer along with spatulas, corn tongs, can openers, plastic spoons, whisks, strainers, mixing spoons, straining spoons, jar lids, bottle stoppers, chicken skewers, sardine keys, jar openers, steak knives, beer openers, melon scoops, tongue depressors, broken wood spoons, corkscrews, lobster scissors, measuring spoons, an ice cracker, a strawberry huller, an ice cream scoop, electric mixer beaters, bottle brushes, cookie cutters, a hand beater, napkin rings, cheese cutters, vacuum bottle tops, measuring cups, bent candles, metal flower holders, ladles, birthday candles, a garlic press, sticks of gum, snarled string, and a Ping-Pong ball.

The drawer will not open. The screwdriver, which is in the drawer, is the tool you need to stick in the crack to lever down the whisk which is pushing up the corn tongs which are gripping the spatula which is jamming the drawer.

Faced squarely with the knowledge that the screwdriver is inside, you either (1) slump at the kitchen table and weep uncontrollably or (2) give the drawer a series of vicious yanks while yelling "Hah!" at each wrench. Neither method works. Trying to force the drawer not only jams it worse, but bends one of the electric mixer beaters. Later it will shimmy against the other beater and make a terrible noise and fling chocolate frosting all over the room.

If the stuck drawer is located underneath another drawer, don't think for a minute that you can open the top drawer to get at the other. The top drawer, containing old ice trays, cutting boards, and a four-sided food grater, isn't just stuck. It's sealed forever.

The best tool for opening a stuck kitchen drawer is a captured World War I German bayonet. Look in your attic. Maybe your neighbor has one. Or you might contact your nearest extremist group.

Once you've pried open the drawer, you'll have to paw through all that junk to find your tools. Make a game out of it. The game is called Kitchen Roulette. The object is to lay hands on a tool before the serrated edge of a steak knife cuts your finger off.

A handy wrong tool for tightening screws around the house—doorknobs, cabinet hinges, etc.—is a small wood chisel. If somebody in the house actually uses the chisel for woodworking it's not such a hot idea to mention that you've been using it as a screwdriver. Quietly put it back exactly where you found it. The same rule applies when you've used a carpenter's level to pound in garden stakes, or a micrometer as a glue clamp.

Maintenance, Repairs, and Repairing the Maintenance

The common small household screwdriver is good for propping windows, hammering tacks, and chiseling wood after the wood chisel has been ruined driving screws. For heavy jobs you'll need a broad-blade screwdriver with a rubber grip. This sturdy tool will enable you to drive a woodscrew almost flush with the surface before the notch strips out and the screw can't be turned either way. Don't try to pull it out with a claw-hammer; the screw won't budge and you may break the claw. You could use the other end of the hammer to smash down the screw, but the surrounding wood will become overantiqued. A hacksaw will cut off the protruding portion of the screw, if you don't care about saw marks marring the surface. The screw can be drilled out, but the job is difficult. At any moment the drill may slip, and the bit will go into the wood and break off. Then you'll have to get the bit out. And a claw-hammer won't work on that, either.

Sometimes it's better to nail two pieces of wood together. At least you can get the nail out easily. That's because the wood splits when you drive a nail in it. For hammering nails, all sorts of tools can be used. The flat side of a pair of pliers makes a popular ineffective hammer.

Hammers, through misuse, also make ineffective hammers. Used to kill ants on the sidewalk all afternoon, a hammer develops a rounded head and is no longer good for driving nails. It is fine for cracking ice in a plastic bag, though, if you get your kicks climbing in plastic bags and cracking ice.

(Ice picks are not used on ice. Ice picks are for punching extra holes in belts and watchstraps. They are also for chipping putty, for transfixing bulletin board mes-

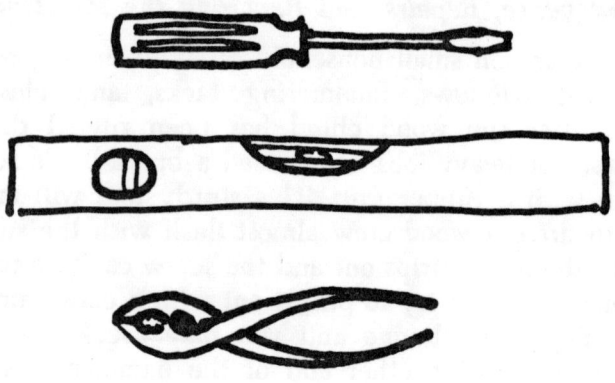

Hammers

Extra Belt-Hole Puncher

Glue Clamp

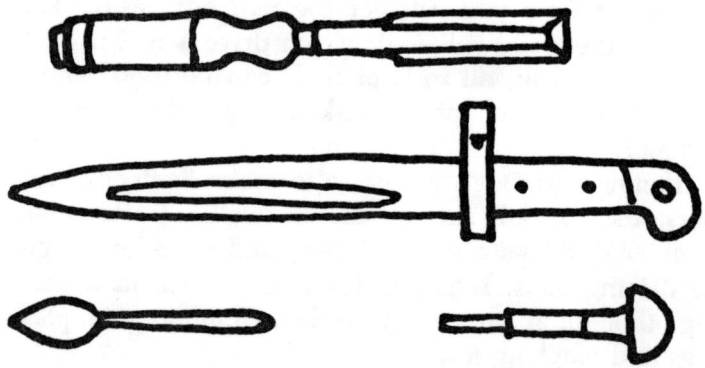

Screwdrivers

Maintenance, Repairs, and Repairing the Maintenance

sages, and for detecting dry rot in boats. If you insist on picking at a block of ice, use either a crowbar or a putty knife.)

Large carpenter's hammers are good for driving little picture hooks right through the wall, and for making holes in other things you don't want holes in. If you try to drive large nails with it you'll soon get a forearm cramp, and you won't be able to let go of the hammer. Until your hand unclenches a few days later, you'll have to take the hammer wherever you go. This is a fairly unnerving experience, especially if the cops are looking for a hammer murderer.

A handy thing to have around the house for accidentally breaking things is a vise. Used for many repair jobs, it makes more repair jobs if you turn it just a shade too tight. Common uses of the vise include flattening curtain rods you're trying to shorten, scarring old picture frames you're trying to re-nail, and pulverizing pottery you're trying to glue.

When using a vise as a clamp prior to fastening, drilling, cutting, etc., you need a minimum of three hands. Each of the two pieces to be lined up requires a hand, and a third hand is needed to close the jaws. People who have less than three hands sometimes foolishly try to line up the two workpieces and crank the vise. It can't be done. If you have only two hands, you must summon a small child to work the crank. He will be delighted. He will jump to his assigned task. He will spin the crank. He will crush your fingers.

Many home projects require measuring. Some even call for accurate measuring. A six-inch pencilbox ruler is fine for determining the length of the splinter in your hand, but for most jobs you'll need something longer.

Two popular measuring devices are the flexible metal rule and the folding wooden rule.

When measuring with a folding rule, make sure it is unfolded all the way and perfectly straight. If it is sort of zig-zaggy you won't get an accurate reading. Wooden rules are fragile and the ends sometimes break off. When using a broken ruler, be sure to add on the missing inches.

One nice thing about a wooden ruler is that you can sit on a warm pile of lumber and make various interesting designs with it, including a perfect six-pointed star.

A metal rule is designed to pull straight out of its case and stay stiff until you reach out to measure something; then it collapses in the middle. A spring winds it back in its little case. Push a button, and sometimes it will zip right back in. Don't push a button, and sometimes it will zip right back in anyway. A flexible rule is full of surprises.

The metal rule is considered to be more accurate than the wooden one, at least until the numbers wear off. After that, your best bet is probably a warped yardstick.

Keep children away from flexible and folding rules. Kids like to duel with them, but they can hurt themselves. To prevent fool cruel rule duels, make tool rules.

As noted previously, pliers can be used to hammer things with. But they're really better for not gripping things with. The reason you can see light between the jaws of most pliers is because they don't close properly. They are made that way so you won't accidentally crush an insect.

For not picking up small things, it's handy to own a pair of needle-nosed pliers with jaws you can see light

Maintenance, Repairs, and Repairing the Maintenance

through. For fine work, of course, you need tweezers with jaws you can see light through.

Slip-joint pliers have a clever mechanical arrangement that allows you to widen the jaws so that when gripping something the ends of the handles snap together and pinch your palm. A quick shift of the axis, and you're back to an ordinary pair of pliers with jaws you can see light through. Wire-cutting jaws at the bottom of the "V" will gnaw through a paper clip in less time than it takes to send the clip out someplace to be cut.

Wrenches of various types are sometimes used instead of pliers. But for certain gripping jobs you can't beat a good old pair of slip-joints. It's too bad they're in the kitchen drawer.

Glue Time

Most adults, and all children, break things around the house. If the broken thing isn't too large, like a wall, the pieces should be gathered up and carefully placed on a shelf to await Glue Time.

Children look forward to Glue Time, but for adults it's something they can either take or leave alone, like cleaning out the sink trap.

You can tell that it's Glue Time when the pieces of broken lamps and toys and crockery start sliding off the shelf and breaking into smaller pieces.

Shout "Glue Time!" and the children will swiftly clear the kitchen table, breaking the sugar bowl, while you fetch the glue. It is best to keep bottles and tubes and cans of glue in one large cardboard carton. You run a slight risk of the bottles leaking and gluing each other in there, but if you don't keep all your glue together you'll spend all of the Glue Time looking for glue.

After today's unread newspaper is spread on the table, all the broken items, including a pile of ceramic chips identified as a "horsie Daddy will make well again," are laid out for inspection.

As anybody who has messed around with glue knows, different adhesives must be used for different materials. (Except fingers. All glue sticks fingers together. Unfortunately, there's no stuff that will glue kids' elbows to their sides. The glue companies probably have it, but are keeping it off the market.) The popular epoxy cement, for example, is excellent for replacing ears on porcelain rabbits, but will not glue tails back on plastic

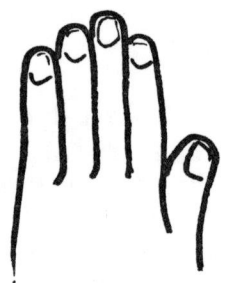

Glued Hand
(Showing Fingers Lined Up Properly)

Irish setters. If you use epoxy on an Irish setter the tail droops, and while you're trying to straighten it, your hands get sticky. If you don't watch out, you'll find both hands tightly glued to a tailless plastic Irish setter. It's hard to get emergency help on the telephone. Pushing

Maintenance, Repairs, and Repairing the Maintenance

the receiver off with your nose is easy; so is dialing with a pencil in your teeth. The hard part is *convincing* people.

Epoxy cement, which comes in two tubes, is not to be confused with model cement, which comes in one tube, only there are two different kinds. One type of model cement works for balsa wood airplanes, and is used by people who like to fasten little sticks together and spend the next twelve hours peeling their fingers. The other kind is plastic model cement, and this works fine on tails of plastic Irish setters and plastic blue dinosaurs. Both kinds of model cement leak out of the tube when you're not looking, and the stuff dries in a twinkling. It seeks out corduroy pants. If you try to get it off, the cordur comes with it, and only the oy is left.

Contact cement is used for bonding large surface areas. It should not be used if you have a quick temper. One mistake with contact cement, and you've had it. You prepare both surfaces, let them dry thoroughly, and then carefully put the surfaces together. It fuses on contact. If you've failed to line up the thing correctly it's too late, because you can't budge it. A crooked kitchen countertop is worse than no countertop, as a woman will remark every day in the year.

Tub and tile caulking compound, called "calk" for short, is an adhesive used to seal around tubs and shower stalls. If water is leaking *out* of your wall tiles, you've got a plumbing rather than a gluing problem. If it's raining at the time, check for a roofing or a siding problem.

Rubber cement is best for gluing paper to paper, or paper to walls if you don't supervise the children.

White glue comes in plastic bottles with caps that glue

The Complete Book of Pitfalls

themselves to the bottle after use. You have to cut open the bottle, and then the glue dries up. A lot of this glue is sold, and you can see why.

Brown glue also comes in plastic bottles, and is made from real horsies. Under no circumstances should this fact be mentioned during Glue Time.

White and brown glue are used for sticking pieces of wood together, like building blocks and pianos. It is best to use glue clamps on wood. There are two types: the wrong kind for the job, which you own; and the right kind, which you don't.

When you tighten clamps, excess glue squeezes out. It must be wiped off carefully with rags. Children like to grab the rags and run around the house, snapping them at each other and covering themselves with glue. Later, they hide the rags in upholstered chairs.

Glue Time always brings new challenges. A boy will ask you to mend his favorite rock. Don't ask him what he broke the rock *on*. Concentrate on one problem at a time. Look through the glue box and see if any of the labels mention rocks. They probably won't.

The best bet is an all-purpose preparation, usually sold as separate cans you mix together. The stuff is demonstrated in hardware-store displays showing a golf ball glued to a bottle glued to a hubcap glued to a stick glued to an iron stand.

Following directions, scoop out both cans with a spoon and mix the material on a board until it (and you) reach a uniform gray color. Then lather both pieces of the broken rock, and stick them together. Leave it to dry overnight, wirebrush yourself, and go to bed.

When you pick up the rock the next morning, the

Maintenance, Repairs, and Repairing the Maintenance

halves may come apart. But man, that stuff can really glue a spoon to a board.

Plumbing and Heating

Although "Plumbing and Heating" is always a single category, plumbing is not heating. Sometimes, because of the plumbing, you have no heating. That's why plumbers are more important than heaters. You rarely phone a heater to fix anything, even if you have no plumb. However, you do call a plumber to fix a heater. Try to keep things straight.

Unfortunately, plumbers are rarely available. They have a busy schedule racing sports cars, buying and selling Thoroughbreds, tending to their yachts, and entertaining at the big house on the hill. Thus you'll have to do your own plumbing and heating.

The most common plumbing problem is a leaking faucet. It probably needs a new washer. Those are little hard rubber discs which seat themselves and shut off the water if they happen to be in the mood. To replace a washer you must take apart the faucet. But first you must turn off the water supply to the faucet by closing the little valve under the sink. These valves are placed at a handy height for little children, who often sneak into the bathroom and turn the water back on just when you've gotten the faucet all apart. This causes a lot of yelling and sloshing around.

Children also like to turn *off* the water. If you get just a trickle of water, or none at all, don't start checking through your whole plumbing system. Make the reliable

The Complete Book of Pitfalls

Homeowner's Assumption, which is "The kid probably did it," and check the sink valves first.

Copper tubing is used in modern plumbing systems, and with a few simple tools you can extend and repair lines yourself. All you need is a solder, flux, steel wool, and a hand torch. The torch should be a small propane-fueled device; not one of those long things used by prison guards chasing convicts through the swamp.

Clean the surfaces of the parts to be joined, apply the paste flux, stick the parts together, and heat with the torch until the solder melts and flows freely. Feed it into the joint, wipe off the excess, and let the whole thing cool. Keep your inquisitive hands off the pipe if you want to avoid agony. A hot copper pipe never looks hot; neither does the end of a propane torch.

After you get the hang of it, you'll find it's fun soldering lengths of copper tubing to elbows and tees and valves and couplings. It's hard to stop though, and before you know it, the basement looks like a jungle-gym. There have been cases of people trapped in their own plumbing, so keep an extra propane tank handy to melt your way out in an emergency.

Repairing existing copper water lines on the basement ceiling can be rewarding, if you think of hot solder down your neck as a reward. It is important (and also impossible) to drain all the water from the lines before working on them. Heating the pipe turns some of the water to steam and you find yourself working over your head with a hot torch, melting solder, and steam. Like repairing locomotives underway, the job is technically interesting but not much fun.

A plumbing system extends outside the house. You will find that the well, well-feed pipe, septic tank and

Maintenance, Repairs, and Repairing the Maintenance

lines, assorted drains, etc. will all have to be dug up at one time or another. Tile drains will break and water will flow in the cellar. Water in the cellar is caused by excess water, flowing in the cellar. The pump will fail. The disposal system will "back up," and there's nothing like raw sewage to put a damper on a patio party. The important thing is to think ahead. While these systems are uncovered, draw careful diagrams so you'll know exactly where to dig next time. It's a common misconception that plumbers and well-drillers can always locate original installations. People who bury things never remember where. Why do pipeline companies trim wide strips through the woods wherever transmission lines are buried? So they can remember where the pipe is, that's why.

Pipes in a home plumbing system regularly self-destruct. Those silly cartoons showing people being sprayed in the face with water from broken pipes, or wading knee-deep in the basement, are correct in every detail.

In the United States there are many kinds of home heating systems, all of them still in the experimental stage. These systems tend to work better in warm weather when they aren't needed. They cease functioning when it gets cold outside.

Hot water, steam, electrical, and hot air systems are controlled by thermostats installed in the wrong part of the house. A popular place to put a thermostat is in the kitchen where it will be fooled by the cooking stove into shutting off the heat in the rest of the house. Another common thermostat location is directly above the cellar light switch which has a pilot light to show when the cellar light is on. While you're down in the cellar the pilot light will heat up the thermostat. The thermostat will panic, and issue orders to close down the heating system. Thermostats aren't very bright.

In recent years there have been some interesting advances in ceiling-heating systems. On cold days, you put your easy-chair up on the dining-room table and it's quite comfortable. With this type of heating system, you get used to having a red face and blue ankles.

Heating systems concealed in the flooring (red ankles, blue face) are also gaining in popularity. Over a few seasons the floor dries out, enabling you to rearrange the floorboards any way you wish. Puzzle fans will enjoy working with parquet floors.

Many people keep quite warm and comfortable all winter by running around trying to get heat. Apartment dwellers run down the stairs to berate the superintendent. Homeowners run down to the cellar to look at the furnace. Kids yell down the hot-air registers. Everybody runs around banging on pipes and radiators, a practice which started when somebody noticed that pipes clank by themselves when the heat is on.

Sometimes, but not very often, you can fix the heat yourself by turning a valve on the radiator or baseboard unit. But the valves are usually painted fast. Painters always paint heat controls so they won't turn. It's just one of those things painters do.

If you find you can turn a heat valve, don't get your hopes up. It will probably come off in your hand. The landlord will say you broke it. "It just came off" is one of those obviously true statements nobody believes.

Follow plumbing repair procedures for fixing the piping part of heating systems, but keep away from boilers because they hiss and rumble and boil and creak and

Maintenance, Repairs, and Repairing the Maintenance

blow up and things like that. Like repairing locomotives underway, the job is technically interesting but not much fun.

For working with heating ducts, see the section on sheet metal work and blood transfusions.

Try to familiarize yourself with your entire plumbing-heating system before trouble starts. Do it sometime between yesterday when the tub drain sprung a leak and tomorrow, when the hot water heater collapses. Go down in the basement and look at all the pipes and ducts running every which way. Stop those silly hysterics; get hold of yourself. Feel each pipe. If it is hot, it is a hot water pipe. If the pipe is cold, it is either a cold water pipe or a hot water pipe not working.

Figure out where every pipe goes, and what it does. (No, "leak" is not a function.) Next, get a stack of baggage tags, write down each function, and tag each pipe. Finally, move your family to some sensible mountain-spring location in the tropics.

Repairing Toilets

Flush the toilet and watch the water. If it runs straight down the sides of the bowl, the fixture is probably an economy model. If you can see separate streams, it is of a better grade. If the streams swirl, it is a quality bowl.—*The Time-Life Book of Family Finance.*

Although there are lots of toilet jokes, toilets are not funny. As the above passage indicates, toilets should be taken seriously and may even serve as a yardstick of

The Complete Book of Pitfalls

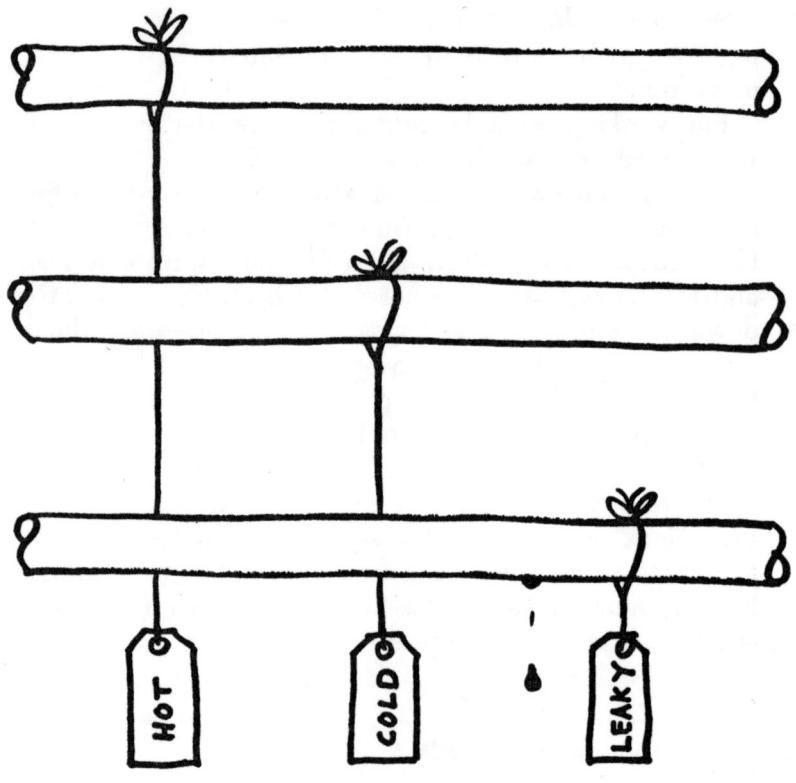

Properly Tagged Pipes

social standing. Next time a guest uses your bathroom, think of him carefully watching how the water goes. Word that you have straight-stream economy plumbing gets around the neighborhood fast.

Much has been written about repairing toilets (though goodness knows why), and the phrase "simple mechanism" is frequently used to describe that awful assemblage of levers and floats and rods and gurgling

Maintenance, Repairs, and Repairing the Maintenance

things inside the flush tank, the thing mounted on the wall behind the toilet proper, or toilet improper. But anyone who has tried to fix anything inside the flush tank (Rule 1: Roll sleeves way up) knows that the mechanism is extremely complicated. What's more, it doesn't seem to have undergone technical improvement since it was invented, some time between Fire and The Wheel.

There are people who pretend to know how to fix toilets, but you'll notice that their technique consists of jiggling the lever. That's not know-how; that's faith-healing.

In many cases, toilet-tank problems may be ignored. You can get used to gurgling. The pleasant sound of running water helps some people sleep. It is impossible to take the top off the flush tank anyway, because everything that won't fit in the medicine cabinet is piled up there.

A common problem with the toilet bowl is clogging with foreign matter, such as a teddy bear. ("When I pulled the handle he just disappeared!") Relax. The first rule in toilet emergencies is Don't Lose Your Head.

To extricate a bear who has fallen victim to a quality bowl maelstrom, use either of two special tools. One is a large rubber suction-cup on the end of a stick, known in the provinces as a "Plumber's Friend." You work it up and down in the bowl, while swearing. The device is really more effective for relieving your own tensions than it is for solving the problem.

The other, preferred, tool is a straightened-out wire coat hanger with a little hook in the very end. Wire coat hangers aren't much good for hanging coats because they bend, and the coat slips off in a heap. But they're excellent for almost everything else.

The wire will follow the toilet bowl's twisting curves until it reaches the bear. Then you snag him with the hook, and slowly draw him back to the land of the living. He will probably need major surgery, but another toilet tragedy will have been averted, and you can go back to the more important business of watching the water.

Appliances

You fight a losing battle when you try to repair and maintain household appliances. There are too many of them, and new ones are being introduced all the time. You're so busy acquiring that you have no time for fixing. A luxury appliance becomes a basic necessity after you've seen it demonstrated on television for a month. Or after your neighbor owns one for an hour. (Times change. Can you imagine Great Uncle Max the Famous Turkey Carver, may he rest in peace, being handed an *electric* carving knife? "Just push the button, Uncle Max, the gadget will do all the rest for you.") Keeping track of all these whirring buzzing blinking appliances is hard enough; to keep them all in working order you'd need your own full-time live-in incompetent appliance repairman.

When manufacturers aren't bringing out new things like battery-operated bookshelves, they're busy introducing new models of old appliances. Washers and dryers and washer-dryers are getting like cars: If you don't get this year's model you lose face. The new model is much harder to repair. That's because the company's research and testing division made the horrifying discovery that a few people were fixing the old appliances themselves. Responding to the crisis with Yankee ingenuity, the firm introduced a new model with rivets instead of screws so you couldn't get it apart easily. If you did manage to punch out the rivets, you'd find a sealed "Lifetime Motor, Needs No Oil" inside. What they're really talking about is the lifetime of the *appliance,* a lot shorter with dry bearings.

Many manufacturers produce nothing but discontinued models. They hurry to get a device on the market so they can stop making it. Even if all your present working appliances are the type that can be taken apart and fixed if they break down, you live with the sad knowledge that you will be unable to get parts.

If the appliance stops working, you know the dreary sequence of events. You take it back to the store. The clerk looks it over with a somber expression—a friend of the family about to notify the next of kin.

"How old *is* this?" he asks, putting you on the defensive. Naturally you can't remember. He flips the switch a couple of times and shakes his head.

"I think my grandmother had one of these once. They stopped making them—oh, I don't know when. We wouldn't have any parts for it of course. We'd have to send it back to the factory in Nome." When you ask him how long it will take, he says about fourteen weeks, maybe longer if the dogs can't get through. Then he steers you over to the new appliances, tomorrow's discontinued models.

Be advised, then, that repairing your own appliances is a discouraging occupation. But if you're willing to fight the unbeatable foe and dream the impossible dream

The Complete Book of Pitfalls

(everything working exactly as advertised) you can occasionally pull off a minor miracle and restore an ailing appliance to health. Some trouble-shooting tips:

Electrical appliances don't work when they're not plugged in. (If you have an appliance that keeps running after you pull the plug, get out of the house fast.) Trying to operate an unplugged device is a common household frustration. While you're trying to cuff a hair dryer into action, a child will point out that it isn't plugged in. It's exasperating, but there's nothing you can do except plug in the dryer and cuff the child.

When a plugged-in appliance won't work, check the outlet. It does no good to peer into the socket. You can't see electricity. Remember when you were a kid and thought electric wires were hollow and "electric" ran through them like water? And you poked a pin in the socket and got a silent shock that scared you almost as much as your mother yelling at you for poking a pin in the socket? Being able to feel electricity but not see it puts the whole business in the twilight zone. That's why Aunt Agnes goes around making sure each outlet has a plug in it, so the electricity won't "leak out" and run up the light bill. After all, if a faucet can leak, why can't a socket?

When someone tries to explain electricity the mystery deepens. Early in life you were introduced—perhaps at a party—to the terms "alternating current" and "direct current." They made no sense at all. What does direct current do, go right to jail without passing go? How can alternating current go first one way and then the other? That's ridiculous. If current alternated, what would happen when you turned on your vacuum cleaner? Ask an

Maintenance, Repairs, and Repairing the Maintenance

electricity expert these questions and he brings out a little piece of paper and draws wavy lines, a real help.

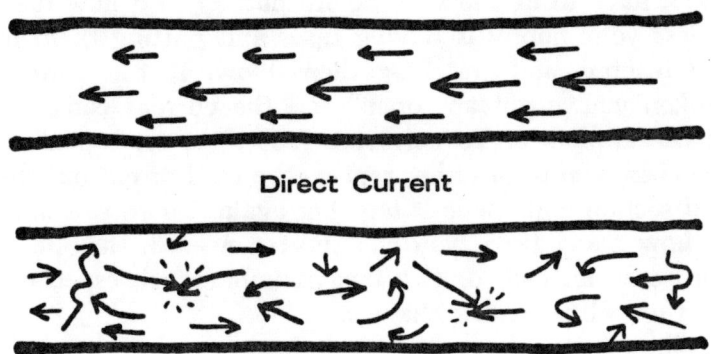

It's easier on your nerves if you just think of electricity as Magic, and go on from there. The electricity is either in the socket or it isn't. In the case of the plugged-in-but-won't-work appliance, the next step is to check the outlet by plugging in something you know works, like a lamp. If the lamp lights, the socket is "good" and the appliance is "bad." This simple test is far more effective than the common practice of scurrying around the house with the doubtful appliance, plugging it into every outlet. Especially if the appliance is a refrigerator.

If your test shows the current supply is okay, maybe the appliance cord is bad. See if it's in more than one piece. Look for frayed places, especially where it enters the appliance, and at the plug end. Constant twisting and rubbing of the cord can expose or break wires. So can throwing the steam iron at somebody without unplugging it.

Inside the cord are two wires. If the wires touch, a "short circuit" occurs. This blows the safety fuse and you'll have to fix the wire before putting in a new fuse, unless your hobby is buying fuses and putting them in the fusebox and watching them blow. If the wire is broken you've got an "open" and the current can't get to the appliance. To correct a "short" or an "open" in the cord, you must either replace the cord or cut out the bad section and splice it together again. There is a limit to how many times you can shorten a cord, though. A cord only an inch or two long is impractical, especially for things like electric shavers.

When installing a new cord, hook up the plug last. If you don't, some kid will stick the plug into a handy live socket while you're busy at the other end inside the portable dishwasher. Suddenly, you'll be a lot busier.

Tie a knot in the wire before fastening the ends to the plug's terminal screws. The pros use an underwriter's knot, but even an overwronger's knot is okay as long as it protects the ends from strain when the cord gets a sudden tug.

Broken wires in the cord or inside the appliance can be soldered together. As in plumbing work, you've got to clean the surfaces to be joined. But soldering wires is a more delicate operation, involving a soldering iron or a "gun" instead of a torch. Use a solder that has a resin core which acts as flux. Heat up the joint and let the joint melt the solder. Carefully remove the gun without disturbing the wires. Let the joint harden before handling the wires.

When working with a soldering iron, you can keep it out of the way but handy by making an eye-bolt bracket and fastening it to the kitchen table. The hot iron will

Maintenance, Repairs, and Repairing the Maintenance

hang down over the edge and you can work efficiently until the dog catches fire.

Appliance switches sometimes go bad. Switches of standard sizes and shapes are stock items, and can be replaced more easily than special parts built for the appliance. If you think a switch is bad, try unplugging the appliance, taking off the cover to expose the switch, bypassing the switch with a temporary wire, and then plugging it back in. If the appliance works, the switch is defective. Sometimes cleaning the switch or switching mechanisms will solve the problem. They tend to get gummed up, especially in toasters where the crumbs from last year's English muffins eventually find their way into the control room.

The principal cause of toaster trouble isn't the switch or cord, however. It's diet bread. The diet bread people feel that the best way to reduce calories, in addition to carefully removing all the flavor, is to make the loaf skinnier. You get an interesting surprise when you try to toast your first slice of diet bread. The toaster goes "click" and you reach over for the toast but there's nothing there. The toast is too little to pop up. It is still down in there someplace.

Peering down into your toaster with a flashlight early in the morning is a bad way to start the day. You can see the diet bread curled up in there, black edges wedged against the heating elements. Turning the toaster upside down produces an eyeful of ancient crumbs and burned raisins, but no toast.

The only solution is to pull the plug and then dig around with a long fork until the toast and two of the heating wires break up. Then everything can be shaken out. In winter you can shake the toaster into the bird feeder, but birds on low-calorie toast are a sorry sight. Their ribs show.

Broken heating elements mean you're in for the "we got no parts" routine again. An alternative is to keep using the toaster as is. Many toasters will continue to operate with missing heating elements; it's just that your morning toast will have a fashionable white streak.

An ailing appliance sometimes can be cured without actually fixing anything, which adds to the mystique of electricity. Motor-driven devices can often be hit or kicked to life. Turning a noisy electric clock upside down and letting it run that way a few days often silences it. But it may not be worth it. If the clock is in a conspicuous place, the constant cackling of family and friends will make more noise than the clock did.

Motor-driven appliances need air to keep them cool, and air vents often get clogged with dirt and dust. The motor heats up and burns out. You can eliminate the dust and dirt problem by covering up the motor. But then it doesn't get any air and it heats up and burns out. The answer is to keep motors as clean as possible by getting to them often. It's a job, because you've got more motors in your home than you realize; everything from big ones powering oil burners and water pumps, to little ones that work record turntables and slide projector fans.

If the motor has little oil cups, put oil in them once in a while. Some larger motors have little holes which mean either (1) you should put oil in there, or (2) under no circumstances should you put oil in there. Whichever you do, the electrician who comes later will clap his hand to his forehead and moan.

One important thing about motors: If there's a burning smell, pull the plug and investigate. A burning smell is one of the symptoms of burning.

Maintenance, Repairs, and Repairing the Maintenance

If your washing machine won't work, check the belts. A washing machine is all pulleys and belts. Each belt has its own function, the principal one being to break down independently of the other belts. Sometimes a belt will quietly slip off its pulley and you won't notice anything wrong until you start ironing dirty clothes. On other occasions the belt will break and go click click click Thump Thump Thump WHAP WHAP WHAP, giving everybody in the house heart attacks. To get to a belt you must remove the sheet metal surrounding the washer frame and fiddle with the rusted belt tension adjustment bolt, a three-hour job if you're handy with a cold chisel.

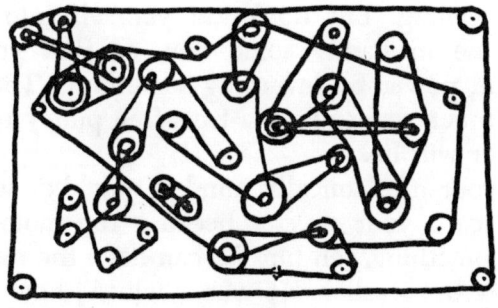

Examine Washing Machine Belts for Wear

An old worn-out appliance is worth less than nothing. When buying a new major appliance, make sure they'll take away the old one, trade-in or not. Make it part of the deal beforehand. If you don't, you'll wake up one morning realizing that you have your very own junkyard complete with all kinds of safety hazards.

People become unwitting collectors of antique appliances by clinging to the mistaken belief that "good parts" can be salvaged from old stoves, refrigerators, etc. In the first place, you won't get around to removing the parts, and the appliance will just sit there gathering dust. Ten years later you'll pay good money to have somebody cart away a piece of junk you've had to walk around for more than three thousand days. The only practical thing you can do with old washers and dryers is to mount them atop telephone poles. With the doors removed, they make giant bird houses.

Old appliance parts aren't "good" in the sense that they can be used for something. If it gives you satisfaction to have a "good" dishwasher timer and a "good" washing machine pulley and a "good" refrigerator defroster unit lying around the house, by all means keep them. Put them in lighted display cases. Hang them from the ceiling. But don't kid yourself into thinking they'll come in handy some day, or that you'll gain wealth and power by inventing something. There never has been much demand for a frost-free pulley timer, and there never will be.

When your mechanically minded neighbor warns you not to discard your washer because the motor can be used for something, tell him *he* can have the motor if *he* takes away the washer. He won't, which should tell you something.

Finally, insist that the old appliance is taken away immediately, in the same truck that brought the new one. Don't fall for that "I'll be back for it later" line. He won't. He'd sooner drive to Nome for parts.

Electrical Work

Doing your own electrical wiring can be exhilarating if you don't have rubber-soled shoes or if you are standing

Maintenance, Repairs, and Repairing the Maintenance

in water. You must follow the home wiring standards contained in the National Electrical Code. Many people worry about whether they are permitted to do their own electrical work. This is the wrong thing to worry about. When working with electricity the first thing to worry about is getting zapped. Keep this foremost in your mind at all times. When your mind wanders from the job at hand and begins pondering the delicate prose of electrical codes, that's when you'll stick your thumb in a fuse socket and get electrocuted or worse.

The National Electrical Code doesn't prohibit a homeowner from working on his own wiring. (Fear sometimes does, though.) Some local electrical codes will give you static, so check with your proper municipal official first. He may want to inspect the job.

Your insurance agent will have apoplexy when he gets word of the project, but don't worry about him. He'll calm down as soon as he can get your homeowner policy canceled.

Installing a new outlet is a common "first project." It involves running new wiring from an existing outlet box to a new receptacle in a new box in a different part of the room. The whole project is a lot more complicated than buying a longer extension cord and moving the lamp, but some people like to do things the hard way.

Before you start, you must decide on the size of wire to use, the type of cable, the size of the outlet box, and the kind of receptacle. Making all those decisions will probably take you all winter and right through into Daylight Saving Time when you won't need the lamp.

The three types of cable are armored (BX), nonmetallic sheathed (Romex), and conduit (Conduit). These contain wires that carry current. The wires come in different sizes. A good rule to follow is to use the same kind of cable with the same size wire that leads to the existing outlet box.

White wires get connected to chrome terminals on the receptacle. Black wires are connected to brass terminals. White wires get connected to white wires; black wires to black. The key to electrical work is segregation. Try to integrate, and it's burn, baby, burn.

Always shut off the power at the fusebox before doing any electrical wiring. Turning off keeps you from turning on.

Depending on the type of cable you choose, you will also need staples, straps, connectors, couplings, and bushings. To make holes in the wall you will need saws and drills and a long piece of coat hanger to fish around with while you're lying on the floor with your face pressed against the baseboard heater.

An ordinary lamp extension cord can be purchased at most stores for less than a dollar.

(Important note: Under no circumstances should regular lamp cord be used for wiring *inside* the walls. Mice who live in there may nibble through the soft insulation down to the bare wires, causing a short circuit. Although this is an effective way to kill mice, it is costly because you have to replace the house each time.)

Another electrical improvement project is installing dimmer switches so you can dial your own level of gloom. These modern devices are highly touted as a good way to cut electric bills, but the savings is offset somewhat by medical bills incurred from falling over the furniture. Incidentally, if your lights become mysteriously dim while you are working on some other electrical project, it doesn't mean that you have invented a dimmer system. It means that there is something seriously wrong.

Maintenance, Repairs, and Repairing the Maintenance

If you happen to be holding a bare wire, you might try letting go of it. If the lights get brighter again, that was probably the trouble.

There are many outdoor electrical projects. You can install floodlights to shine in the faces of guests and make them lose control of their cars in your driveway. You can position the floods so they illuminate your house, giving prowlers a good look inside and preventing you from seeing out. You can install weatherproof outlets so you can entertain your neighbors with outdoor records, radio, and TV this summer. You can install a permanent plastic lighted Santa Claus on your roof with red eyes that blink slightly out of phase. The possibilities of outdoor wiring are almost limitless.

A popular project of many homeowners is installing an outdoor post lamp. A popular project of many vandals is tearing down an outdoor post lamp. A popular project of many homeowners is repairing and rewiring an outdoor post lamp torn down by vandals. And so it goes—plenty of satisfying do-it-yourself work for everybody.

Putting in a post light requires digging, not only for the post itself but for the waterproof UF cable that will run under your lawn between the house and the post. UF stands for underground feeder and utter fatigue. With post lights, there's a lot more digging than wiring. In fact, it's practically all digging. Many how-to articles on installing post lights show a smiling and unsoiled fellow adjusting his colonial lamp with a screwdriver. This is not realistic. By the time you've finished digging, you can't straighten up enough to reach the lamp, and your hands aren't strong enough to grip a screwdriver. All you can do is stay on your hands and knees, crawl slowly back to the house, and curl up with the National Electrical Code.

House Painting

The job of painting your house can be put off for two or three years by squinting. After a while, though, the peeled areas get too large to ignore. It is time to paint.

Painting a house sounds like a big job, but you can do it yourself if you break it down into three distinct phases. They are:
1. Choosing the color.
2. Preparing the surface.
3. Painting.

Many people find they can avoid all the work of Phases 2 and 3 by getting bogged down permanently in Phase 1. Start by examining and comparing color charts. You will note that one company alone offers seventeen shades of green: Woodlawn Green, Balsam Green, Cascade Green, Apple Green, Light Apple Green, Patio Green, Spring Willow Green, Laurel Green, Moss Green, Arbor Green, Chrome Green, Brilliant Green, Park Green, Pale Green, Valley Green, Essex Green, and something called Medium Blind Green which looks exactly like Tropical Turquoise.

The only two patches on the charts with simple names are White and Black. Black is easy to remember because it looks exactly like Essex Green.

Individual paint companies have their own paint names, causing further confusion. One firm's Rust Brown is another's Tudor Brown is another's Oakwood Tan. Only housewives claim to know the difference; only their hairdressers know for sure.

Maintenance, Repairs, and Repairing the Maintenance

New colors, with new names, can be formed by combining two colors on the chart. Thus, Warm Beige is by Beachwood Beige out of Sandstone. New paint names are added to the list regularly; it is only a matter of time before a left-wing manufacturer will introduce Better Red Than Dead.

If you manage to survive the long bout of acute indecision and choose a color scheme for your house, the next step is to order not enough paint and to begin preparing the surface.

Surface preparation involves scraping and wire-brushing, the same thing you do to yourself after you've finished painting. Remove all peeling paint and loose spider webs. On window frames, dig at old putty until you hear a "click" and a jagged line appears across the windowpane. Remove the glass with a cloth-covered rock. The remaining putty can then be scraped away without finesse.

Exterior painted surfaces suffer from eight common ailments, and they are easy to remember: Blistering, bleeding, scaling, wrinkling, checking, and peeling are the same things that happen to your skin the first weekend at the beach. The other two—mildew and mold—happen the first rainy weekend at the beach.

Blistering, scaling, and peeling are caused mainly by moisture between the inner and outer walls. This problem must be corrected before painting or you'll just get blistering, scaling, and peeling all over again. It sounds discouraging, but it's really a blessing in disguise. Until you correct the moisture problem, you don't have to paint. A man can enjoy many seasons of uninterrupted golf if he convinces his wife that some strange thing is wrong with the vapor barrier. "With condensation like that, Honey, buying paint is just throwing money away."

The Complete Book of Pitfalls

The wrong kind of primer paint, or no primer at all, can cause scaling, bleeding, or wrinkling. Your local paint store man will be delighted to help you select the right primer. It's in those cans in the locked showcase— a special mixture containing diamond and platinum chips to hasten drying.

Checking occurs on old paint exposed to extreme weather. Checking looks like antiquing. Many people spend lots of time and money getting a surface to look like that. It would be a shame to paint over that lovely checking, wouldn't it? If that argument fails, you've got to scrape off all the paint and apply fresh primer and a finish coat.

Little spots and larger splotches identify mildew and mold. Sometimes the surface is covered by a web of wavy dark lines. Moldy and mildewed houses are too damp. Check to see if your house is located under a waterfall, or if plants are blocking the sunlight. A large beanstalk next to the house will sometimes cause a mildew problem. After cutting down the stalk and eliminating the dampness problem, buy a paint containing a mildewcide. Don't get discouraged and commit mildewcide. That's killing yourself with an overdose of fungi, and it's a bad way to go.

The job of taking off paint can be made easier with a liquid remover. It softens up the paint so you can transfer it directly from the house to your own body. Unfortunately, there is no paint remover to remove paint and paint remover mixture from your skin. For a while it's a horrible, tacky mess, but eventually it dries on you. Over the years it will come off. By peeling, checking, wrinkling, scaling, bleeding, and blistering. Stay out of damp places or you'll get mold and mildew, too.

If using liquid paint remover doesn't appeal to you, an

Maintenance, Repairs, and Repairing the Maintenance

electric heat lamp may be substituted. It loosens the paint so you can scrape it off with a putty knife. Notice how scraping is always involved, even when you use a blowtorch to burn off paint. Unless you hold the torch too long in one spot. Then igniting is involved. And phoning. And fleeing. And firefighting. And questioning.

After the surface has been prepared, painting can be put off because it is either too wet or too dry or too hot or too cold. Most days fit one of those categories. Many homeowners find they can paint only a few days each year—in the spring just after it gets warm enough but before the wasps get too numerous, and in the fall just after the wasps pack up and before it gets too cold. Painting the house that way may take six or seven years. In the meantime, there is always the hope that you will be transferred to a new community with a painted house.

Sometimes, alas, the Stratford Blue sky will shine down on the Hothouse Green lawn for several glorious days. It will be perfect painting weather, and you must get out the ladder and actually start to paint.

Begin painting at the peak, and work down. There is a logical reason for this. When you fall, the streak from your brush will cover unpainted surface all the way down. Try not to cover work you've already done.

Trim is another matter. Say you are painting your house red, with yellow trim (Rose Red and Rose Yellow). If you paint the red part first and then the yellow part, you get yellow spots on the red. If you paint yellow first, it gets red spots on it. Windows get both red and yellow spots. The large splashes of red or yellow on the windows, which look as if a paintbrush has been tossed against the glass, are caused by wasps flying at you while you're up on the ladder.

Sometimes, under the eaves, you will accidentally

paint a bat. Bats hide in obscure nooks during the day until they are painted, and then they flutter away cursing. Try to avoid painting bats. A red bat with yellow trim is a disturbing thing to see, and to think about.

House painting can be a family affair, and children like to help. Give them their own little paint brushes and paint cans. Let them work on their own special projects, like doorknobs and the electric meter.

Interior Painting

In many ways, painting inside is worse than painting outside. Weather and insects cannot be used as an excuse not to paint. Choosing colors is more difficult because more colors must be chosen. The more rooms, the greater the opportunity for color clashes. Ceilings are often painted a different color from the walls, requiring precise "cutting in" where wall and ceiling meet. You get a stiff neck painting a ceiling, and your glasses get covered with spots. Those who don't wear glasses get their eyes spotted.

Light-colored paint makes the ceiling seem higher. Darker colors lower the ceiling, and you have to scuttle around the house in a half-crouch.

Surface preparation is more complicated indoors. You must remove pictures, mirrors, switch plates, door hardware, outside cabinet hinges, and sometimes even lighting fixtures. Anything not removed must be covered up. Ceiling fixtures may be dropped, and then covered with newspaper and tape. While you are taping the paper around the fixture, the black wire may come loose and make a big fat spark. When that happens, covering

Maintenance, Repairs, and Repairing the Maintenance

leads to igniting and phoning and fleeing and firefighting and questioning.

Every piece of furniture and every inch of carpet must be covered. If there's a tiny hole in the drop cloth, that's where the paint will spill. Plastic sheeting has largely replaced cloth as a covering. It is inexpensive and works fine as long as you don't panic and thrash around when you get caught in it.

Walls and ceiling must be clean and all cracks must be patched before you start to paint. The experts say to widen hairline cracks with a scraping tool or beer opener in order to create a better channel for the patching compound. Do this at your own risk. Widening a crack can dislodge a chunk of wall which was holding up a bigger piece of wall which in turn was supporting the ceiling plaster. Thus a surface preparation problem can easily become a house falling down problem if you're not careful.

Preparing windows for painting is a matter of choice. You can either mask the glass (a masked window can be identified only by its fingerprints) or you can very carefully paint the frame and mullions with a small brush. Most do-it-yourselfers prefer the latter method because it permits them to toss the word "mullions" into the conversation later ("I had a terrible time with the mullions"). Exterior painters like the sound of "soffit." If you can manage to paint both on the same day you'll score impressive cocktail party points ("I tell you Charlie, when I close my eyes all I can see is mullions and soffits").

When paint slops over on the glass, don't try to wipe it up. You'll wipe some of the paint off the wood and then you'll have to paint it again and the paint will slop

The Complete Book of Pitfalls

over on the glass and you'll go round and round all day until acute mullioncholy sets in. Let the paint dry on the glass, and you can remove it with a razor blade at a later date. It's a good project for those hours between the time you've got the car all packed, and the time the rest of the family is ready to leave for vacation.

Painting may be done with brush or roller. Rollers are excellent for large flat surfaces, including the ceiling. Many handles have sockets which allow you to attach extension poles. The socket comes loose when the roller is directly overhead.

Brushes come in all sizes and prices. Experts who tell you to buy a good brush because it will last longer don't take into account the fact that you won't get around to cleaning the brush. Most sensible people collapse immediately after painting a room. The brush either dries out and is thrown away, or it is put in a jar of turpentine until the turpentine evaporates a year later and the brush dries out and is thrown away.

They say a good brush holds more paint and does a smoother job. But in actual practice the only difference you'll notice is that the bristles come out of a cheap brush. If a bristle is deposited on a conspicuous surface, you've got to pick it off and paint over the spot. But that doesn't happen too often; the eye-level part of the wall is usually painted with a roller. In most cases you can just leave the bristles where they are. If a guest gets down on all fours to check the baseboard paint for bristles, he's being rude and you shouldn't invite him back.

For many years, the best paint brushes were made from natural hog bristles. Nowadays almost all brushes have nylon bristles, even though there appears to be no shortage of natural hogs.

Maintenance, Repairs, and Repairing the Maintenance

There is an approved method of dipping a brush into a paint can. Professional painters work from a half-full can and dip only a third of the bristle length into the can. Then they slap the inside of the can with the brush and withdraw the exact amount of paint, without spilling a drop. This method may be correct, but it's dull. Amateur painters prefer to brighten the day by using the Erupting Volcano Technique, wherein the paint flows steadily down the side of the can all day, gradually covering the village.

Open a gallon can and stir it vigorously. That will start the paint flowing over the edge and down the outside. Then dunk the brush down until paint just touches your knuckles. Withdraw the brush and wipe off the excess paint on the edge of the can. Some of it will run down outside. Dip the brush in again to get a little more paint on, wipe some of that off, and you're ready to start painting. One advantage of the brush-dunking method is that when you're finished whatever it is you're painting in the house, the floor will be painted, too.

When painting a room, begin with the ceiling and work across the narrow part. Make a strip about two feet wide and then start on a new strip before the first one dries. Don't drive yourself into a frenzy, though. If it dries, it dries. After another four or five coats you'll never see the streak.

Paint walls in sections, working from the top down. Brush on the paint the way it's easiest for you; painters themselves can't agree on technique. Some prefer short horizontal applications, others favor a criss-cross stroke, still others paint obscene words on the wall and then fill in around them.

If you want to paint with a roller, do the corners first with a brush or edge roller. Then you can make short work of the remaining expanse of wall. A roller also makes larger letters.

When you've completed a section, go over it lightly with the brush or roller to produce a smooth finish. You'll have to touch it up again tomorrow, however. If you put up "wet paint" signs everybody will feel the wall. If you don't, everybody will lean against it.

Cleaning up after painting is a simple matter. Throw away the brushes immediately, and that will get rid of the guilt over not cleaning them. Gather up and discard the drop cloths before they get so stiff you have to saw them up in little pieces to get them out of the house. Place the lid back on the paint can. The little gutter around the rim will be full of paint. When you hit the lid with a hammer, a funny thing will happen.

Spray Painting

Paint stores sell little pressure cans of spray paint. While satisfactory for small jobs, the cans aren't very economical. It would cost you roughly three quarters of a million dollars to paint your garage that way. However, spray painting can be done on a large scale. If you have a large scale you want painted, spraying is the answer. You'll need to rent a commercial paint-spraying outfit, the kind that runs on compressed air.

Don't use your vacuum cleaner as a paint sprayer, no matter what the salesman told you. It's a messy job, and you won't be pleased with the little black specks and bobby pins on the side of the house.

The secret of successful spray painting is covering up, or "masking," everything you don't want painted in-

Maintenance, Repairs, and Repairing the Maintenance

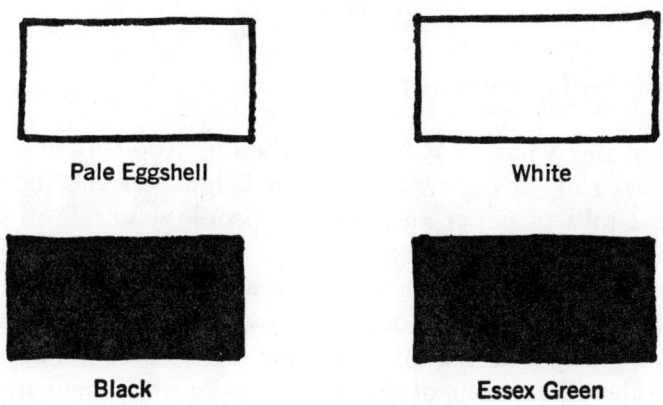

Four Popular Colors

cluding Mr. Seligson's black Cadillac down the street. Even on calm days, the spray drifts everywhere. Don't spray on windy days. You'll paint the next town. It will be easy for you to tell which way the wind is blowing; that's where all the yelling people will come from. Wind broadens the scope of a painting project. You start out painting a lawn chair and wind up having to do the whole house.

Wear covering clothes, and a mask to keep you from breathing in the larger droplets of paint. Any remaining exposed portions of the body should be covered with grease. If you wear glasses, cover them with grease, too. You won't be able to see much, but the paint will come off later.

It's not a good idea to spray-paint inside the house. If paint fumes don't get you the explosion will. If you have interior furniture to be painted, take it outside and spray it. Several thin spray coats are better than one thick one, if you don't mind layers of flies.

Wall Covering

Over the years, starting even before Adolf Hitler, paperhanging has gotten a million laughs. In the movies, great rolls of paper curl up over people who fall off ladders covered with paste as dogs chase cats around the room. It's what advertising copy writers call "a laff riot."

People who have done their own wallpapering rarely even chuckle at the antics on the silver screen. They remember great rolls of curling paper causing them to fall off ladders on dogs and cats covered with paste. (Never mind what modifies what, you picky grammarians; *everything* was covered with paste.)

In recent years the job of wall decorating has become a little easier, but paperhanging is still nothing to be sneezed at. Especially when you're trying to line up the edges.

The most difficult job is preparing the surface. The very thought makes the brain cringe. So many more jobs would get done around the home if you didn't have to "prepare the surface" first. By the time you get a surface prepared, all enthusiasm for the project at hand has disappeared. Remember Uncle Percy who invited you and all the other kids for a Sunday drive? As you gathered around he said, "First we must wash the car. . . ."

Many people have such severe hangups about preliminary work that they flee from place to place all their lives, leaving a trail of unprepared surfaces behind them. Or else they tackle the job without preparing the surface. That's possible in a paperhanging project, but it's not a good idea. Chances are you'll run into trouble.

Maintenance, Repairs, and Repairing the Maintenance

Putting new paper on old paper is risky unless the old paper is still adhering firmly. And you know it isn't. Deep in your heart you know the old paper is loose and cracked and awful.

Too many layers of wallpaper can give you a closed-in feeling. Many city apartments have been papered over so many times that there's no room in the rooms. A good rule of thumb is that if both elbows touch walls—and you're standing in the room the long way—you should remove all the old wallpaper and start all over again. However, if you have unusually long elbows, you might possibly get away with one more layer of paper.

To remove old layers of wallpaper you need old clothes, a wide putty knife, and a compulsive urge to destroy. You loosen up the paper either by soaking it with hot water or using a wallpaper steamer. You rent the latter at a paint store, not a shipping office.

Do-it-yourself books say the job is messy, but that it goes fast once you start. Only the first part is true. Have you ever heard of a messy job going fast? You'll be steaming and soaking and scraping and slopping and slushing and slogging around that room for days. Only two things will relieve the boredom. The first is the layer by layer discovery of what hideous taste the previous tenants had. The other is the prospect of finding a million dollar bill or an original Van Gogh between the wall and first layer of paper, a logical hiding place for money and paintings.

As you wield the scraper, be careful not to gouge the walls. Not only will the Van Gogh be ruined, but you'll have to fill up the holes before you put on the new paper.

Cracks and holes should be filled with spackling compound and sanded smooth after dry. The next step is to apply a coat of wall size, a gluelike substance which seals the surface and also fills in small depressions. Like your ears and eyes.

Materials you'll need for papering are a paste brush and bucket, a sponge, a plumb line, chalk, a stepladder, a yardstick, scissors, razor blades, a smoothing brush, a seam roller, and the same putty knife you used for wall-gouging.

Instructions that come with the wallpaper tell you that a long, clean, flat work surface is essential for preparing the paper. The illustration shows a smiling man standing at a banquet table, brushing paste on an endless strip of paper. He is wearing a necktie. Do you know anybody who wears a necktie when he applies wallpaper paste?

Face the fact that paperhanging is a grubby job, and that you won't have enough space to work in. If you're lucky, you'll find room someplace to set up a lone card table, and you'll make do with that. Afterward, the table won't be any good for card-playing. Each time you shuffle, the bottom card will stick to the table. You'll have to play with an incomplete deck, stopping every few hands to steam and scrape cards.

There are formulas for estimating the amount of paper you'll need, but they don't take into account dog and cat damage. Your best bet is to supply the dealer with your room dimensions, plus window and door measurements, and a list of household pets. The dealer will give you enough rolls of paper to do the room. Make sure he has more of the same pattern on hand.

Start papering next to a door. (Don't paper over the door.) From the door frame, measure out a distance of one inch less than the width of the paper, and make a

Maintenance, Repairs, and Repairing the Maintenance

mark. Then, using the chalked plumb line, snap a perfectly vertical line against the wall. Then go to bed. That's quite enough for one day.

When you return to the room several months later, maybe someone will have already papered it. Or taken away the rolls of paper and applied a decent coat of whitewash. If not, you've got to start hanging the wallpaper.

Cut off a piece from the roll the distance from floor to ceiling plus about eight inches to allow trimming on the top and bottom. Then lay the paper face down on the work table and start brushing paste on the back, as the remainder of the roll falls off the table into the fresh bucket of paste.

After plucking out the roll and flinging it against the wall in a blind rage, finish applying paste to the first strip and then start on exposed parts of your body. Remove your clothes and cover yourself completely with paste. Now you are ready to (1) go out in the street and dance, or (2) apply the first strip of paper to the wall. If you choose to be dull and hang paper, here's the technique:

Carefully line up the first strip so the edge touches the chalk line, and smooth it out against the wall. It helps if you apply the paste on one half of the paper's length first, fold it over loosely paste side to paste side, and then do the same thing with the other half. It also helps if you don't lose your head as you're trying to hold the paper up against the wall and unfold it at the same time.

Once the paper is lined up, use a smoothing brush or damp sponge to flatten out the strip and remove bubbles and wrinkles. Then carefully trim off the top and bottom with a razor blade, and wipe off the excess paste.

Some paper comes with untrimmed edges, and you use

a long straightedge to trim off the selvage. That's done while the paper is on the table. Next time, get smart and buy paper already trimmed.

Each succeeding layer of paper is applied to the wall just a tiny bit away from the preceding one, and then sort of nudged over in place so it matches up. Press the edges down with the seam roller. Before you put paste on the next strip, the books say to hold it up against the wall to make sure it will match up with the other piece. To do this, just pull the roll apart until one hand is up against the ceiling molding and the other hand is against the baseboard. Then go out in the kitchen and eat a bunch of bananas.

Save leftover strips and use them around windows and doors. Remove wall fixtures and switch plates, paper over them, and then cut out the openings later if you can find them. Some people carefully paper each individual switch plate, making sure it exactly fits in with the wall pattern. This type of person Simonizes the inside of his glove compartment, and fills unused pegboard holes with Plastic Wood.

One kind of paper comes with the paste already applied. You put a water trough on the floor, soak each precut strip in the water for a minute, then slowly pull one end out of the trough, unrolling the paper and climbing the ladder and scratching your nose and lighting a cigarette. The trough gets moved along the floor as you apply successive strips. Try to keep your feet out of it.

When you come to the corner, take the paper around to the next wall about an inch. Before starting on the new wall, make another chalk mark if you can find the plumb bob under all that rubble.

In order to paper ceilings it takes two people, both insane. If you're thinking of papering your ceiling you don't need instructions, you need a doctor.

Today, the home decorator has a huge assortment of wall coverings to choose from, in every imaginable pattern, color, and material. The secret of modern decorating is to apply something that looks like something else. There are plastic coverings that look like cloth, cloth coverings that look like tile, tile coverings that look like metal, metal coverings that look like wood, and wood coverings that look like plastic. And vice versa. You can also get fiberglass panels that look like real rocks cemented together. So far, they haven't tried to make real rocks look like anything else, but they're working on it.

You don't need water, paste, or tools to apply many of the modern materials. You just stick them on, after peeling off a protective backing. In a jiffy you can cover your walls with imitation bricks, your refrigerator with imitation wood, your windows with imitation chair caning, and your chairs with imitation stained glass windows.

But even with stick-on materials, ceilings are almost impossible to get right. You might try nailing up the fake fiberglass rock panels, though. In this nuclear age, a stone ceiling gives you a sense of security.

Screens and Storm Windows

Climates do exist that offer neither bugs nor cold weather. These places are nice to visit but you wouldn't want to live there. Too dull. For one thing, you'd miss the semiannual ritual of wrestling with screens and

The Complete Book of Pitfalls

storm windows. This healthy activity acts like a spring and fall tonic, making the blood course through the veins and causing the face to take on a rosy glow. Sometimes purple.

In recent years lightweight metal sash and "combination" screen–storm window units have been introduced. These make the changeover job easier, but it's still a tiresome chore offering ample opportunity to break glass, rip screening, fly into a rage, or fall out of a window.

If you plan to fool around with screens and storm windows, it is important to know the difference between the "sash," which is the framework around the glass or screen, and the "frame," the opening in the building where the sash fits if you're lucky. The two terms are easily confused, especially when stuck together to form a "framesash," or a "sashframe." Know your sash from your frame. When two people are working on windows, one inside and one on a ladder outside, precise communication is essential. Shouted instructions like "Hit the sash!" "Pry the board!" and "Kick the frame!" invite disaster unless each person knows exactly what the other is yelling about.

If you like puzzles, switching around the old-style wooden storm windows and screens offers a nice challenge. No two frames are alike. In contrast to the modern age of standardization where everything is the same size and universally shoddy, the old windows were sound but different. Houses were erected by master carpenters who expressed their individuality by fashioning one window a little bit wider and another not quite as tall. Sometimes they just forgot previous measurements. By the time they got around to the front door it was hard to remember what size they'd made the back one.

Maintenance, Repairs, and Repairing the Maintenance

After the window frames were set in, individual screens and storm windows had to be built and carefully fitted. Life was difficult for the proud new owner of this kind of custom-built home. Braving fall winds, he had to stagger around the house with each storm sash, trying it on every frame for size until he found the right one.

These hardy pioneers soon grew weary of the trial-error method, and began to develop their own identification systems to match sash with frame. Perhaps the most popular was carving a different Roman numeral on each set. (Roman numerals are easier to carve than Arabic numbers, and just as efficient except when you try to jam screen No. 9 into frame No. 11.)

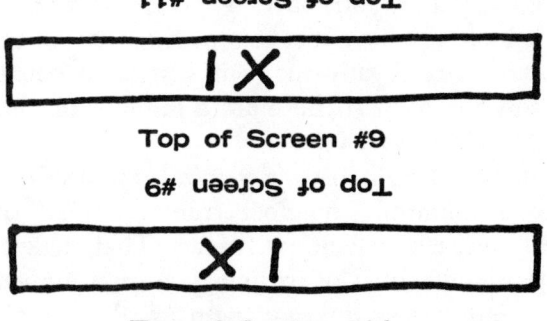

Digging marks into the sash had two major drawbacks. After a few paintings the marks filled up and disappeared. Also, since wood swells it was often necessary to plane down a sash. When Grandpa discovered he had planed off his Roman numeral the children had to be hustled out of earshot.

Sash-carving became obsolete with the introduction of tacklike markers with raised numbers on the head.

The Complete Book of Pitfalls

You pounded one tack into the window frame, one into the screen sash, and the third into the window sash, cracking the glass.

The invention of the wooden "combination" storm and screen door greatly simplified that changeover chore. You no longer needed to remove the whole door; you just used a screwdriver to remove an inset and replaced it with either a screen or a window, depending on the season and how far behind you were in your chores.

Entire screen porches have been fashioned from wooden combination doors fastened edge to edge. The advantage is that you can turn a screen porch into a glassed-in porch by just switching the insets. The disadvantage is that you have a porch with two dozen doors all looking alike. Just one of them is the real door. This is a serious disadvantage if you have cocktail parties on the porch, or if there are a number of children in the house in a hurry to get out.

In many modern houses, door and window frames are made of aluminum. The door frames are all the same size, and so are the window frames. That makes the insets interchangeable, providing you can unfasten the little knurled screws holding them in. You usually can't, and the screen stays in all winter. Be very careful when handling the new aluminum-sash screens. The screening is of extremely thin material, evidently to keep the cost down. Flies make dents in it, and sometimes the screening will tear under the weight of a climbing spider.

New hardware has been introduced. Old-style screen doors had long springs fastened to them so the door would close with a bang and drive Aunt Agnes up the wall. Children gave the door an extra flip out of deviltry, and learned that a knot tied in the middle of a worn spring restored zip. A different kind of closing device is used on the modern metal combination door. A tube-shaped gadget fastened near the top of the door goes "hssssssss" and ever so slowly and gently eases the door almost shut. Turn a little adjustment knob at the end of the tube and the door slams shut like a mousetrap. The difference in settings between "hssssssss" and "bang!" is infinitesimal, and you need the sandpapered fingertips of a professional safecracker to get it right.

A Weekly Garbage Schedule

Keeping garbage and papers off your lawn, driveway, and the street is a difficult task in the winter. The rapidly changing weather works against you. So do the garbage men. The best way to deal with the garbage-scattering problem is to follow a schedule. It runs something like this:

MONDAY

Garbage men back their truck over your shrubs and lawn, stopping when the truck hits the garage. They empty your garbage cans, and also take away any wastebaskets you've left out there. They leave the big garbage can with no bottom; the one you've been trying to throw away for a year. After skimming your garbage can lids around the property, Frisbee-style, they drive away.

Go out and carefully set up the empty cans and put

The Complete Book of Pitfalls

the correct lids on them. Place the cans where they can't blow away.

TUESDAY

High winds pick up the empty garbage cans and blow them away. The lids blow off in the opposite direction.

Go out and retrieve the cans and lids. Set everything up again, except the can that was run over by a car. Place the smashed can next to the bottomless can where the garbage men will be sure to see it next week and not take it.

WEDNESDAY

Dogs knock over one full garbage can, scattering garbage over your lawn, and letters from your creditors over the lawns of your neighbors.

Go out, pick up the garbage, and put it back in the can. Your neighbors will take care of the letters.

THURSDAY

The wind blows the lids off the garbage cans. Rain falls in the cans. The temperature drops, the water freezes, and one garbage can bursts.

Go out and break up the frozen garbage with a crowbar. Pick up the lumps and put them in a cardboard box. Put the burst can in the no-pick-up pile.

FRIDAY

A rapid rise in temperature melts the frozen garbage in the cardboard box. The box gets soggy. The box collapses. The garbage spills.

Go out and scrape up all the garbage and put it in the

Maintenance, Repairs, and Repairing the Maintenance

one remaining garbage can. Carefully reaching on tiptoe, place the lid atop the pile, like a hat.

SATURDAY

The wind knocks over the can. Dogs come and spread the garbage around. Snow falls.

Go out and right the empty garbage can. Find the lid. Put it on the can. Where is all the garbage? Under the snow, that's where. Leave it there, and pray for a long winter.

SUNDAY

A blazing sun melts all the snow, exposing soggy garbage everywhere.

Go out with all your wastebaskets and use them as emergency garbage cans. Shovel all the garbage into the wastebaskets. Weigh them down with stones from the front walk.

MONDAY

Garbage men back their truck over your shrubs and lawn, stopping when the truck hits the garage. They throw garbage, wastebaskets, and stepping-stones in the truck. They leave the bottomless garbage can, the smashed garbage can, and the burst garbage can. After throwing the remaining lid back and forth, Frisbee-style, they climb in the truck and drive away.

Go out and buy new garbage cans and new wastebaskets. Set the new cans next to the garage where they can't blow away. Go in the garage and discover two dozen paper bags of garbage you forgot to set out for the garbage men. Fill up the new garbage cans, and put the overflow in the new wastebaskets. Set all the cans in a neat row. Hear the wind rising in the trees. Listen to the sound of the distant dog-pack. It's Monday, and you already have a full week of garbage on display.

Sheet Metal Work

If you have never worked with sheet metal, you have a hand-opening experience ahead of you. The important thing to remember with sheet metal projects—installing chimney flashing, fabricating heating ducts, etc.—is not to bleed to death.

There are numerous incidental expenses connected with doing your own sheet metal work. Before you start you should have on hand:

1. Tin snips, large and small.
2. Gloves.
3. A "brake," or device for bending sheet metal.
4. Tourniquets.
5. Sterile catgut.
6. A clean six-foot-long table, illuminated by a bright light.
7. A surgeon, anesthetist, and registered nurse standing by at all times.
8. Eight pints of blood.
9. A direct phone line to the Blood Bank in case more is needed.
10. All the medical and accident insurance anyone is willing to sell you.

With time, luck, and an adequate number of transfusions you may become proficient in sheet metal fabricating techniques. Then, of course, it's no more dangerous

Maintenance, Repairs, and Repairing the Maintenance

than working with rusty razor blades or broken glass, and can be just as rewarding.

When Your Mailbox Flunks

If you are new to the rural area, you'll probably go all to pieces when your roadside mailbox fails inspection. In the first place you had no idea that mailboxes were inspected, and secondly, you never realized so many things could be wrong with your mailbox.

Oh, the shame of it all, when you fetch the mail and find a green and white official mailbox rejection sheet, POD Form 4056. There are eighteen little blocks for the mailman to check, including one that says "Your box is not an approved box."

At the top of the form, in italics, it says "Your Mailbox Needs Attention." Nearby are pictures of two mailboxes. One is all battered and leaning; the other straight and neat. To drive the point home, the Post Office Department takes a leaf from children's look-think-circle books, and asks: "Which one looks like your mail box?"

You know you're in disgrace when you find several of the following blocks checked:

"The door needs attention.

"The signal flag needs attention.

"Box must be located so carrier can serve it without leaving vehicle.

"Your box is not waterproof.

"Your box should be raised———inches.

"Your box should be lowered———inches.

"Your box should be on the right hand side of the road as traveled by the carrier.

The Complete Book of Pitfalls

"The approach to your box should be kept free of snow.

"Your box is too near the road.

"Your box is too far from the road.

"Your box should face the road.

"Your box should be securely fastened to its support.

"Your box should be leveled, and the post firmly planted.

"A new post for your box should be provided.

"The approach to your box should be filled and properly graded and kept unobstructed at all times.

"Your box should be painted to prevent rusting.

"Your name and box number must be printed not less than one inch high on the side of the box visible to the carrier as he regularly approaches it or on the door if the boxes are grouped."

At the bottom of the form is a blank space for "Other Irregularities." It is impossible to think of any.

If you installed your own mailbox, chances are that the "Your box should be lowered" block will be checked. A too-tall mailbox, which makes the rural carrier strain himself reaching up or worse yet leave his vehicle, is a common offense.

Here's what happens: You dig the hole, put in the post, and start to shovel back the dirt. When you tamp the dirt around the post, some of it gets underneath and pushes it up. As you continue to fill and tamp, the post slowly and sneakily rises higher and higher. By the time you're finished, it's illegal.

To pass inspection, you must dig out the post and make the hole deeper, or remove the mailbox, saw a few inches off the post, and then fasten the box back on again. Make sure it faces the road. The Post Office Department has a good point there.

Maintenance, Repairs, and Repairing the Maintenance

Preventive Maintenance

Preventive maintenance is replacing shoelaces before they break, and who wants a guy like that around? If something works the way it's supposed to, or works any way at all, sensible people are content to let it alone and catch a little rocking chair time, perhaps cuddling a pitcher of martinis.

Newspaper household columns tell you to examine your rain gutters for wear, and your sash cords for frayed spots. But it's a lot easier to examine the gutter after it falls down. And by that time you may have moved. The new owner will be stuck with the job. There is also the possibility that an all-out nuclear war will take place before the gutter needs major repairs.

Inspecting a sash cord involves taking the window frame apart after first getting the window unstuck. But what's the use of fixing a sash cord on a window that's stuck closed, anyway?

People who look for trouble usually find it, and finding trouble is a discouraging business. Take a close look at the family car. See how it's rusted all along underneath the door? See the big brown spot on the fender? Poke at it with a screwdriver. See how you made a hole in the fender? See how you can make the hole bigger by just tapping around the edges? See all the other little brown spots? And see that little springlike piece hanging down by the back wheel? See how you can ruin your day when you start inspecting things?

The same thing can happen with your home if you're not careful. For instance, look up under the roof, just to the right of the attic window. Didn't something move? Right where it looks like there's a little hole. It is a little hole! Looks like some animal might have—yep, by gum, there's a squirrel! He just came out of the hole. There's another one. He seems to be biting at the hole. He is. He's gnawing at it to make it bigger, that's what he's doing. Man, they're probably having a ball up there in the attic! It's a wonder they haven't chewed through the ceiling. Come to think of it, there was a funny noise last night in the bedroom closet. . . .

Look at that shade tree. It's so nice to have one next to the house. Wonder why it doesn't seem to be giving as much shade this year? Some of the leaves are turning brown. The limb must be dead. Limbs. Half the tree is dead. The part over the house. The bark doesn't look good on the other part, either. It's peeling off in big chunks. . . .

Talk about peeling, look at that paint! Whole east side of the house. Especially near that window, the slanty one. No, the window is straight; the rest of the house slants. Wonder why? Maybe it's those rotten boards. Two, no five, of them are rotted all the way through. In places you can see the insulation. In some places you can't see any insulation. You don't suppose the animals. . . .

Enough. Close your eyes, just relax. Listen to the sounds of nature. Chirp chirp. Tweet tweet. Warble warble. Squeak snick. Squeak snick? That's a funny sound. Almost like a motor going bad. Squeak snick.* It *is* a motor going bad. Someplace in the house. A noise like that sets your teeth on edge. Enough to shake the bricks loose from the chimney. Hey, speak of the devil! Take a look at that chimney. . . .

---

* *Not to be confused with snick snick, which is a tiddlywink inside a washing machine water pump.*

Maintenance, Repairs, and Repairing the Maintenance

As you can see, it's better not to examine things too closely. A snooping-around system of preventive maintenance will make you a nervous wreck in short order. If you insist on fixing things before they give up the ghost, try the burst-of-energy approach. Say you are oiling a tricycle wheel because it won't turn. You complete the job. You have the oilcan in your hand, and your hands are covered with oil. You might as well go around and oil all the doorknobs and hinges, plus anything else you can think of like the folding ironing board and the TV stand wheels and the kitchen drawer tracks. Then, instead of cleaning your hands on an old rag which later will set your house afire by spontaneous combustion, wipe them on tools. The oil will keep the tools from rusting.

The same principle can be applied to painting. Its a chore to get everything ready, but once you finally get around to painting a wall or a piece of furniture, the job goes quickly. Suddenly you've finished it. You don't want to put all that stuff away, and so you find yourself wandering around with a wet brush, looking for something else to paint. Don't fight this impulse. Paint everything, stopping only when you collapse or run out of paint. Later, you'll get some static about the walls, table, ceiling, chairs, and floor all being the same color. Don't let it bother you. In a condescending tone, reply, "Preventive maintenance."

You mustn't get involved in the seasonal maintenance projects that do-it-yourself publications are so fond of assigning ("Rivet your sidewalks together before frost sets in!"). These spring, summer, fall, and winter checklists just make you feel guilty. You know you'll never get around to doing any of the things on their list because you're too busy working on your own Laggard's Checklist.

The latter involves routine tasks, runs at least two seasons behind, and contains these typical reminders:

SPRING

Put up bird feeder Grandma gave the kids last fall.
Remove Christmas tree from front porch. Lean it against back of house.
Unfasten circle of wire from front door. Sweep porch.
Winterize garden tractor and power mower.
Rake leaves.
Examine galoshes on radiator in back room where you put them to dry in February. Scrape off galoshes.
Gather up remains of pup-tent.
Bring wheelbarrow and outdoor barbecue grill under cover. Examine for rust spots. Examine for spots not rusted.
Remove yellow bug bulbs from outside light fixtures. Replace with white bulbs.

SUMMER

Drag Christmas tree from back of house to edge of garden.
Take down storm windows, put up screens.
Store winter clothing.
Put away sleds and ice skates. Untangle vine from skis. Put skis away.
Take string of colored lights off spruce tree.
Change clocks to Daylight Saving Time.
Remove burlap from shrubs.

Maintenance, Repairs, and Repairing the Maintenance

FALL

Roll Christmas tree just over neighbor's property line.
Weed garden.
Put up birdhouse Grandma gave the kids last Christmas.
Finish setting up portable swimming pool for kids.
Start spring cleaning.
Get lawn mower started.
Remove white bulbs from outside lights. Replace with yellow bug bulbs.

WINTER

Burn debris at edge of your property, including neighbor's Christmas tree of two seasons ago, the one he rolled over on your side.
Take down screens, put up storm windows.
Scrape remains of rotten jack-o-lantern from porch.
Look over borrowed garden tools, but don't return them. Neighbors don't need them now.
Bring in lawn chairs.
Put away summer clothes.
Check dogs for ticks.

III

HOME IMPROVEMENT AND RAINY-YEAR PROJECTS

A Cotton-Picking Hobby

From time to time, it's good to depart from routine home maintenance work and tackle a special project. A special project is something that isn't really essential but you do it anyway for the satisfaction of showing up the people who told you it couldn't be done. Sometimes it can't be done, but you try anyway because you're not too bright.

An interesting project is putting a new wick in the table lighter. It takes many months but it can be done, if you have patience bordering on stupidity.

Before you start, be advised that there is a hidden cost. Although a new wick costs practically nothing, you will need glasses by the time you have finished the project. If you already wear glasses, you will need a stronger prescription. While you're working on the project your eyes will bulge and your head will ache.

A cigarette lighter needs a new wick when it won't light and you can't find a little piece of string sticking out the top. If it makes you feel better, you can make it spark a couple of hundred times, change flints, and soak it with lighter fluid. But it still won't light, and eventually you'll have to go to the store and buy a "wick kit." Pronounce it carefully; otherwise the man will sell you croquet set parts.

[93]

The Complete Book of Pitfalls

The kit contains a coil of white cord, not quite as long as a football field. You'll also find a "wick inserting tool," a tiny piece of wire the color of the rug. One end of the wire is bent to form a triangle. That's so you can get a better grip on it when your hands are trembling.

The first step is to unscrew the fill-cap on the bottom of the lighter. This can only be done with a dime. A screwdriver blade is too narrow, and pennies and nickels are too big. If you don't have a dime, give up the project. You've no business owning a lighter, anyway.

After taking your ten pennies to the bank, having them changed to a dime, and using the dime to unscrew the cap, you'll be able to peek into the little hole in the lighter. You will see cotton. The instructions say:

"Take a pair of tweezers and remove all the cotton from inside the lighter."

Two important steps must be taken at this point. First, put the instructions in a safe place because you won't be needing them for some time. Secondly, find a place to work that has adequate light and space. A small warehouse with a skylight is excellent.

A cigarette lighter contains an amazing amount of compressed cotton. It must be picked out wisp by wisp, and it all must be saved. The wisps expand, and soon you'll be covered with cotton. Children will think you're a giant boll weevil. It is best to divide the cotton into large piles, leaving narrow aisles so you can get around the room.

After a week or two, the tweezers will no longer reach far enough into the lighter to pick out the cotton. The little wire tool is then used as a pick. You'll be so busy you'll hardly notice the change of seasons.

When all the cotton is removed, prepare to insert the

Home Improvement and Rainy-Year Projects

new wick. The instructions say that the wick must be poked into the wick-hole from the top of the lighter. This is hard to do because the wick is larger than the hole. The little wire tool is used to poke it down, a fraction of an inch at a time. Physical and mental stress is greatest when trying to start the wick on its slow journey into the lighter.

The directions note that when one-quarter of the wick is inside, a third of the cotton must be put back inside the lighter, from the bottom. After that, the wick and the cotton are alternately poked in.

Soon a daily routine is established: Push the wick in during the morning hours. Poke cotton all afternoon. Drink and sob in the evening.

You may experience a temporary setback when the job is almost done, with the wick sticking up about a quarter of an inch. You may accidentally give the wick one poke too many and it will disappear inside the lighter. Start taking all the cotton out again.

Before you know it, the long year will be over and you'll have the wick sticking up just the way you want it. Then you simply fill the lighter with fluid, and screw the cap back on—if you can find a dime.

Concrete

Now and then, everyone has the urge to whip up a batch of concrete. A strong and practical building material, concrete will last for a long time, or at least until freezing weather. It has many uses around the home. A concrete path will keep children from wearing out the ground. A cement patio will keep guests outside where they belong. A ten-foot wall with spikes will control the new neighbors.

The standard formula for mixing concrete is one part cement, two parts sand, three parts gravel, and four parts plastic toys if little kids are helping you. Concrete can be mixed in anything, but it is better to use a container you don't care about, or hate.

To make concrete walls, sidewalks, planters, hitching posts, footballs—anything with a definite shape—you will need to build a "form" first. The form is made of wood, and form-building is governed by a Universal Law which says: "No matter how strong you make the form it won't be strong enough and wet concrete will ooze out and spread all over everything and you will be helpless no matter how much you yell and run around." The Law is hard to believe and hard to memorize, but do both.

The larger the project, the more dramatically the Law will be demonstrated. Say you plan to make a concrete swimming pool in your back yard under the shade of the old washline. First you dig a pit with vertical sides. Then you build forms, braced and crossbraced, designed to shape the inside walls and contain the concrete mix while it hardens.

For a job that size you need wet-mixed concrete brought in by truck. You order it by phone and after they get finished snickering they'll take your address and get a rough idea of how much concrete you'll need.

The ready-mix men arrive with tears in their eyes and, after looking over your setup and surviving a coughing fit, they assemble sections of metal trough leading from the truck to the pool. For a while, as the truck gushes forth the sloppy mixture and it flows down between the forms and dirt walls, everything goes smoothly. You

Home Improvement and Rainy-Year Projects

poke at it with rakes, and the wall rises higher and higher.

But suddenly, you hear the sound of bulging plywood. (Have you ever heard plywood bulge? It is a terrifying sound.) Then, with the crack of wood and the pop of nails and the snap of braces, concrete flows out from under the forms with a tired sigh. The delivery men put away the trough, paint another little homeowner on their truck door, and drive away.

The concrete, covering the bottom of the pool, is there to stay. After it hardens you remove the forms and tell friends that you decided to "pour the bottom first." Soon you'll start dumping garbage in there. Dirt and leaves and dead branches will follow. Eventually the pit will fill up to ground level, rich in minerals. Many a successful back-yard garden has started as a homemade swimming pool.

For smaller jobs you mix the concrete yourself. Whether you use the formula method or buy a sack of premixed dry ingredients and add water, you run two major risks: mixing too much, and mixing too little. Unlike sex, not enough is better than too much. A half a patio is better than two patios when you only have room for one patio, especially if you have a neighbor who doesn't want a patio.

When you've mixed too much concrete, you have about half an hour to figure out what to do with it. After that you know what to do with it. Dress yourself in protective clothing and safety goggles, get out a sledgehammer, and go to work.

Breaking up concrete in a wheelbarrow is bad because you'll break up the wheelbarrow, too. The same thing goes if you've mixed the concrete in your station wagon. Dump it someplace, quickly. If you are the same lucky fellow whose pool forms collapsed, you'll have the whole pit to dump the leftover concrete in. Otherwise, you'll have to look for a spot. One solution is to have on hand a quantity of eyebolts and empty two-pound coffee cans. You fill each can with concrete mix, stick in an eyebolt, let it harden, and in a twinkling you have handy little canoe anchors.

A word of warning: You may have heard the term "yard of concrete." It is misleading. If you are having ready-mix delivered, don't attempt to calculate the amount needed by measuring your new sidewalk site with a yardstick and then ordering ten yards of concrete. You will risk a heart attack when the truck arrives. A "yard" is actually a "cubic yard," equal to twenty-seven cubic feet.

If that doesn't mean anything to you, think of it as 3,962 canoe anchors.

Room Dividers

Room dividers are gaining in popularity. It's easy to see why. A room divider turns a large comfortable room into two little cramped rooms, disrupting the normal flow of traffic and creating more nooks and crannies to clean.

Room dividers can be built almost any way, and usually are. Some have a solid lower half, and an upper half of grillwork you hang limp artificial plants on. Other dividers are solid floor-to-ceiling partitions which have the additional advantage of blocking off natural light from windows.

Home Improvement and Rainy-Year Projects

If you are an ambitious do-it-yourselfer, you can make a continuing project out of room dividing. You divide a room in your house or apartment one year, re-divide it into four rooms the next, then eight, etc. The smaller the room the more safe and protected you'll feel, especially if you've done any time in prison.

Some people prefer to ease the severity of Cellblock Modern by adding a mural to one wall. It can be a landscape, a street scene, a seascape, or even a large color-tinted photograph of the scene that could be viewed through the window before it was blocked off by the room divider.

If you decide to build a room divider, the first step is to decide which room you want to divide. The next step is to move all the people out of the room, and that's not always easy. Stubborn older people kick up an awful fuss, and cling to the furniture. You have to pry them loose and drag them off while they swat at you with *National Geographics*. Senior citizens don't like room dividers. If you don't believe it, try putting up a screen in front of Grandma and see what happens.

Once the room is cleared—check around for people crouched behind chairs—the next step is to build a frame for the room divider. If a floor-ceiling petition is planned, you can use 2 by 4 lumber and basic framing techniques. Experts say you may use 2 by 3 lumber if the partition won't be loadbearing, whatever that means. You'll have to decide yourself whether you're going to get drunk and lean on it.

A "sole plate" gets nailed to the floor, and a "top plate" to the ceiling. Before fastening them down and up, place a framing square across both plates and mark off where you want the vertical "studs" to go. These should be

The Complete Book of Pitfalls

either sixteen or twenty-four inches apart, depending again on how loaded you're going to be.

In case you didn't recognize it, the framing square is that rusty L-shaped piece of metal the kids used last spring to chop daffodils. Don't worry about all those vague little numbers on the square. They tell you how to calculate the pitch of rafters. If your room divider has rafters, you're in trouble. Check to make sure you have the right blueprints; you may be building a garage in your house.

The studs get toe-nailed between the top plate and the sole plate. Toe-nailing is exactly what it sounds like. You brace the stud against the plate with your foot, and drive a nail at an angle through the stud into your toe. After you do it once, you'll brace the stud with a short length of 2 by 4 instead.

Once the framing is finished and the rug is nailed down permanently, shelves, storage cabinets, hi-fi niches, indirect lighting units, and even fish tanks may be built into the structure. There should be some way to get the fish tank out, though.

If you prefer a smooth-walled divider, you can panel it with a wide variety of materials, or a variety of wide materials. Panels are four feet wide and eight feet tall. Putting them up is fairly easy once you get the knack of toppling over with a panel without hurting yourself.

Care must be taken to line up each panel correctly. Then, using special invisible nails and an invisible hammer, fasten the panels to the studs, finishing off both sides of the partition. Since the panels are large, the job goes quickly. Your new room divider will be completed before you know it. Enjoy it while you can. In a few minutes, you'll realize the cat is missing.

Home Improvement and Rainy-Year Projects

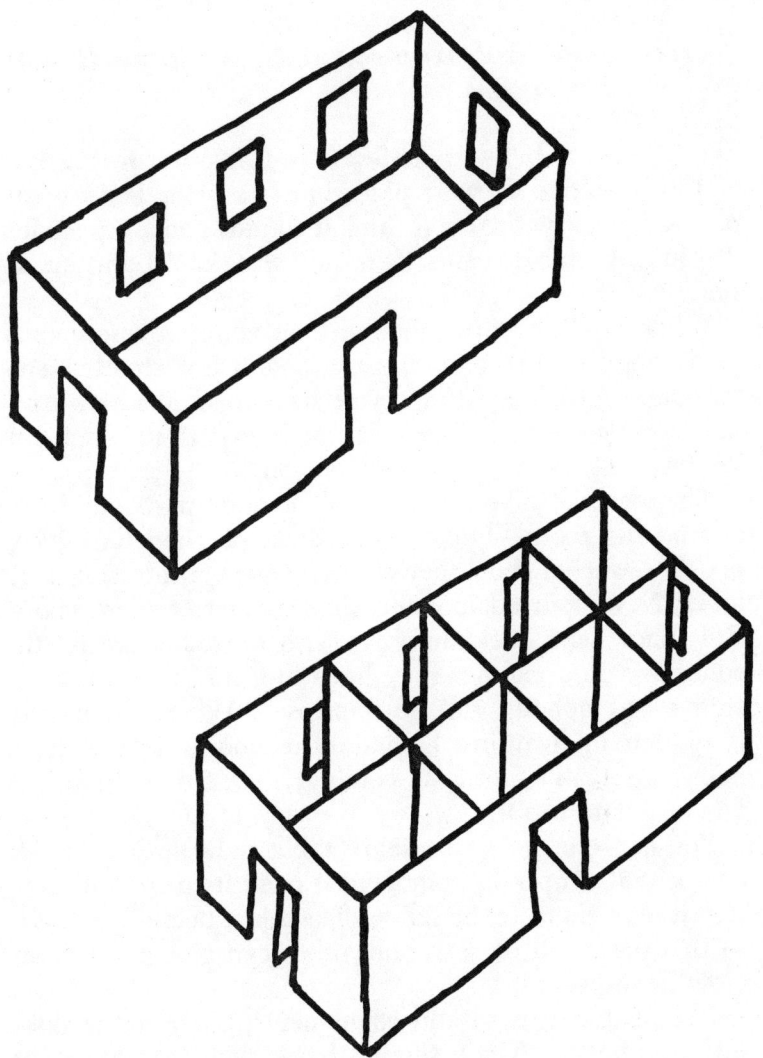

Using Room Dividers

Never a Null Moment with a Sharp Broad Adjustment

The difference between hi-fi and lo-fi is often in the eye of the beholder. If your pad's music system looks complicated, most people will think it sounds good, especially if you get up now and then, adjust a knob, and smile smugly.

While you're waiting for the time you can assemble a really good hi-fi system, you can take a few simple steps to make everybody think you have one already. And you don't have to be an electronics expert to climb on the low-cost, fake fidelity, bandwagon.

The secret of fake-fi is clutter. The more parts you have around the room—lying on the floor, perched on tables, peeking out of bookshelves—the more professional it looks. Never put components in a cabinet. A man whose FM tuner, tape deck, amplifier, and turntable are neatly concealed in a cabinet may have hi-fi and he may have stereo, but nobody will be impressed. When equipment is hidden in furniture behind little doors, people don't know where the music is coming from. To hear stereo, you've got to see it.

You can change an ordinary table radio into a fake-fi component simply by removing it from its case, and putting it on a shelf. It should be placed just below eye level, so that parts can be seen, and tubes can give off a warm glow in the evening.

The next step is to add components, the weirder-looking the better. They should have dials or knobs or switches, or a combination of all three. Stick them here

Home Improvement and Rainy-Year Projects

and there, and string wire from one to the other. Don't conceal the wire; in fact, it's a good idea to position one wire so that visitors must step over it. Make some professionally apologetic comment: "Watch the pre-amp lead, I haven't finished winding the core."

Components are easy to find. Junk shops and junk yards offer a wealth of material. Almost any electrical-looking thing will do. If it can be made to light up, so much the better. Old radios are excellent, and so are old TV sets without the picture tube. (Even out of its cabinet, a picture tube looks too much like a TV set.) Extremely impressive is a car speedometer wedged between your books and connected to another component with a spiral telephone cord. Anchor the speedometer pointer on the dial just to the right of center, about sixty-five mph on most GM cars. This gives you a steady "plus" reading, attesting to the soundness of your music system.

Genuine electronics experts build their own components in aluminum boxes, available in all shapes and sizes at radio supply stores. Get some of these boxes and glue knobs on them. Electronics catalogues offer packages of miscellaneous knobs, some even with pointers. If you want to get fancy, you can get rotary switches with shafts. Drill holes in the boxes, install the switches, and fasten the knobs to the shafts. While music is playing, ask a guest to turn one of the knobs "just a hair to the left." Then say "No, no, too far."

Stretching your arms to turn two knobs at the same time has a good visual effect on guests, especially if you do it with your eyes closed. The fact that listeners can't tell the difference in the sound quality works to your advantage. Your ear is sensitive, theirs aren't.

The Complete Book of Pitfalls

Labeling knobs and switches is a matter of personal choice, and you'll have to decide whether you belong to the "No Information" or the "Obscure Information" school.

Real electronics experimenter-builders never label which knob does what because they *know*. You can create the same impression. The No Information technique works best with a long, low aluminum box containing at least a dozen identical round brown knobs, shoulder to shoulder, with nary a hint as to what they do. If you want to bug the eyes and boggle the minds of friends, put another long box on top, that one full of unmarked toggle switches. Don't worry about anyone touching it; nobody will come near the thing.

Members of the .Obscure Information school label knobs and switches, but with electronics terms that make no sense to the layman. Simple terms like "Volume" and "On-Off" are never used. Get one of those label-makers (see next chapter) and print terms like "Impedance Circuit" and "Grid Leak." You can get a lot of mileage out of "Peak" and "Null." One highly successful fake-fi expert attributes his success with women to an old Heathkit Q-multiplier he found somewhere. Impedance reportedly drops to zero after he goes into a routine of moving closer on the couch, frowning suddenly, and then reaching over to a little gray box on the coffee table and adjusting three knobs labeled "Null Adj," "Peak Adj," and "Sharp—Broad—Null."

Whether or not your equipment is labeled, it may be improved by adding pilot lights. These are red, green, white, or amber jewels that light up when something is not working and should be, is working and shouldn't be, or is supposed to be working and is. You can buy pilot

Home Improvement and Rainy-Year Projects

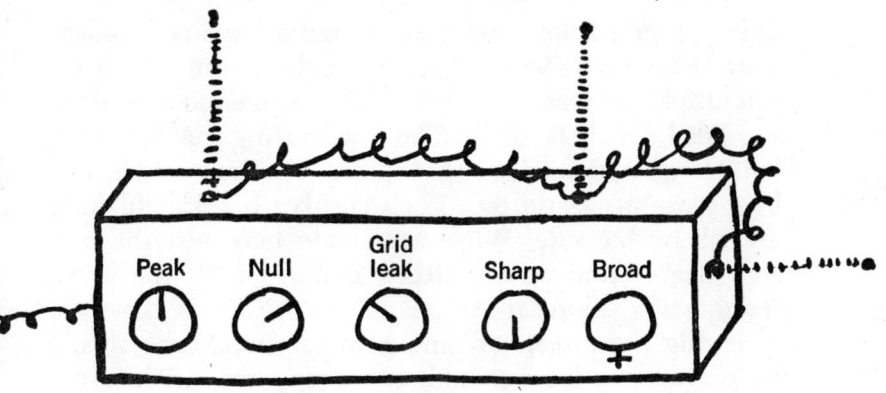

Fake-Fi Control Box

lights that run on house current. You put them in little aluminum boxes, and then run wires to the wall socket. These actually serve a practical purpose. When your lights go off in a power failure, the pilot light will go out, telling you that there's a power failure and that your lights are off.

Just as your electronic equipment should be in plain sight, so must be your speakers. Don't hide them. They should be in boxes, carefully placed so that people have to walk around them. They should look scruffy. A splintered, dirty speaker box means that there is a very expensive speaker inside and that the box was built for its acoustical properties, not for looks.

If you have a monaural system, it can be turned into an excellent stereo system merely by adding a second dummy speaker. A stereo set has two speakers, one on each side of the room. They look alike. Run wires from each speaker to one of the other components, or into the books.

To make a speaker box, tack a piece of dark cloth

tightly over a frame and then wedge a large embroidery hoop behind it so you can see a circular outline. To make a multiple-speaker box, fasten several one-pound coffee can lids behind the cloth. The best-looking speakers have both large and small circles against the front cloth, and beer glass marks on top. Each speaker box should have a knob on the side. When somebody falls over the box, sigh deeply and spend fifteen minutes with the knob, "readjusting the balance."

Setting the proper volume is important. Music should be played just loud enough so nobody can think. Properly distorted, music from one speaker sounds like it's coming from ten. Put little wads of cotton deep in each ear before your guests arrive, turn the gain all the way up, and greet people while nodding and snapping your fingers. Everybody will know you've got a great music system. And you'll never have to worry about conversational lulls.

For a quieter, more intimate evening, the importance of earphones in the fake-fi system cannot be overemphasized. This is the modern way to listen to stereo (the approved technique is to lean back with your mouth ajar and eyes slightly crossed), and if you can get somebody to wire a set of earphones into your lo-fi system it is well worth the trouble. It doesn't matter what it sounds like, and only one earphone has to work. Confronted with a battery of glowing equipment, your visitor will automatically assume one ear has gone bad.

They tell the story of one inventive genius who carried fake-fi all the way to its logical limit. His apartment was filled with old coverless radios, fake speaker boxes, speedometers, aluminum boxes, pilot lights, controls, and wires. And over in one corner of this electronic

Home Improvement and Rainy-Year Projects

haven was a comfortable nook where he would seat his date, and gingerly hand her a set of padded earphones. The chick would put them on, and then he would make careful and delicate adjustments to an odd and impressive-looking device.

Suddenly, an awed and delighted expression would come over her face as she heard music—from a crystal radio.

The Moving Plastic Writes . . .

Labeling machines have become very popular around the home, especially with people who keep forgetting what things are called. These pistol-grip devices shoot out words on a strip of plastic. The plastic comes in assorted colors. You just dial letters, keep pulling the trigger, and eventually an orange word comes out of the gun. You snip off the strip, peel the backing, and stick the word on something.

One widely published ad shows a man firing out EMBOSSED which, on reflection, doesn't make much sense. Does he plan to stick the label on something that is embossed? What? It would seem more logical for the tape to say BANG. Advertising is a funny business. The same ad shows a nearby electric drill labeled JIM WRIGHT, handy in the event of a sudden amnesia attack in the workshop. A glass jar of assorted wood screws is labeled ASSORTED WOOD SCREWS. Evidently Mr. Wright can't see through glass.

The labels do have their practical uses. They identify small parts stored in coffee cans and other opaque containers. On a fusebox, they tell what fuse controls what.

The Complete Book of Pitfalls

They keep pegboard-hung items in their proper places. They eliminate confusion where there are several switches together. And housewives use the labels to tell what's really in those canisters labeled Flour, Sugar, Coffee, and Tea.

Not everything can be labeled. Many useful possessions are hard to describe in short, neat, heavily embossed words. After you fire off a few quick rounds of HAMMER, SAW, WORKBENCH, and maybe MISC BOLTS, you start running into more difficult categories.

For example, there's the shoebox that would have to be labeled STUFF THAT CAME OUT OF THE OLD RECORD PLAYER & SOME RUSTY NAILS. It's unwieldy, and making it cramps your hand.

Another possession that sounds silly in capital letters is CROOKED PIECE OF WIRE TO OPEN SCREEN DOOR WHEN LOCKED OUT, which hangs in the garage next to BEER OPENER FOR OIL CANS ONLY.

And what about that special short steel rod with a jagged edge you always use to hit and pry things with? How do you label that valuable tool without sounding ridiculous.

People save lots of things in boxes and closets for important reasons they can't really explain. These items aren't labeled, either. It would be embarrassing to have somebody else read WORTHLESS BATTERIES, LEAKY PAIL, SEASHELL FRAGMENTS, UNMATCHED EARRINGS, EMPTY BLEACH JUGS, USED FLASHCUBES, or OUT OF FOCUS SLIDES OF KIDS.

Before undertaking a labeling project, take a good look around your home and decide what can be labeled and what can't. There is no excuse for rushing out and buying a labeling machine unless, of course, you own something EMBOSSED.

Home Improvement and Rainy-Year Projects

What Goes Up Must Fall Down

A traditional home project is putting up the Christmas tree. And putting it up. And putting it up. The annual scene is familiar. As the children shout merrily, you stumble through the door with the tree, ricochet off the wall, regain your balance, set up the tree in the corner, step back to admire it, and it falls on you.

There are various scientific reasons why Christmas trees topple soon after you put them up. If you'd stop yelling and consider what is wrong (other than the fact that you're lying under a tree with a face full of needles), you'd realize that you have one of the following problems:

1. Tree stand too small. Each year the stores offer undersized Christmas tree stands that have a base diameter of not more than eight inches. Balancing a room-size tree on this device is a feat to challenge the most skillful of circus jugglers. You must add ornaments two at a time, on opposite sides of the tree. If the cat jumps down from the couch the tree will fall over.

2. Tired weak leg. Larger tree stands are manufactured with one defective leg. It slowly bends and collapses when weight is applied, and the tree falls over. The leg is just strong enough to support the stand alone, while it's at the store.

3. Clamp failure. Some stands have undersized tree-trunk clamps designed to screw into the wood until the threads strip. Then the trunk slips sideways, the tree's weight shifts suddenly in one direction, and the whole thing falls over.

4. Cup metal fatigue. Most stands contain water

cups, large enough to keep a mouse alive for almost a day. The cups help support the tree. Designed to rust out without delay, they collapse and the trunk slips down and the tree's weight shifts suddenly and the tree falls over.

Once in a great while a stand will keep a tree up. But not straight up. The Leaning Tree Horror reduces happy families to tears. You can get a Christmas tree straight one way, but never the other way. Many couples spend the entire holiday period in tense dialogue—"A little more toward me." "Okay?" "No, no, too much." "How's that?" "No, it's not straight this way." "Ow!" "Now it's leaning toward the wall." They never do get the tree straight until they stick it in the garbage can.

You can avoid the leaning tree problem by suspending the tree from a ceiling hook, so that it hangs about an inch from the floor. This method makes the tree perfectly straight, but there is one little drawback. The slightest movement of air makes the tree turn.

After quaffing a few Yuletide toddies, it is unnerving to see your Christmas tree moving. Out of the corner of your eye you can see the lights turn, first slowly one way, then the other.

After trying the hanging tree for one year, most people go back to the undersized base with collapsible leg, bad clamps, and a rusting water cup. A falling fir is better than a sneaky spruce.

Build an Ashtray

Building a bolted-down, nonwashable ashtray will tip the scales in a grim domestic conflict which, although

Home Improvement and Rainy-Year Projects

seldom aired publicly, is one of the coldest of cold wars.

The ashtray struggle is a subtle war between the sexes, and it goes something like this:

A man sits down, lights a cigarette, and looks around for an ashtray. None can be seen; not even one of those awful clam shells which women think are cute and which make the worst ashtrays in the world.

"What happened to all the ashtrays?" the man asks.

The woman answers: "They're being washed."

The man wants to know why. The woman replies, as if to a child, that the ashtrays are dirty.

The man says he emptied two ashtrays that morning. Those two should now be ready for more ashes.

The woman says all the ashtrays are empty, of course. But they are out in the kitchen.

The man asks if perhaps he could have just one of them, since nobody is smoking in the kitchen, and the ashtrays aren't doing much good out there, are they?

The woman looks distressed. She has been very, very busy all day knitting snowsuits and matching underwear for the children and she hasn't had time to wash the ashtrays. They are dirty, she adds.

The man decides to apply logic to the situation—a grave tactical error.

He announces that since he plans to put ashes in the ashtray, it doesn't make much sense to wash the ashtray first. He will just make it dirty again with more ashes. He smiles the slight smile of Perry Mason after a successful jury sum-up.

With a tired sigh the woman says all right, she'll drop everything and wash ashtrays. She strides from the room, with a parting shot that the man is sloppy because he is dropping ashes all over himself. There are sounds

The Complete Book of Pitfalls

of clicking and scrubbing, and of water coming from the faucet at unnecessarily high pressure.

In a short time, the woman brings back an ashtray and clanks it down on the coffee table. She says: "There, it's clean!"

The man lays his cigarette in the ashtray. There is a sudden hissing sound. The ashtray is wet.

This same scene will be repeated endlessly unless some method to anchor the ashtray is found. One excellent way is to start from scratch, and fashion a separate unit of furniture. The parts:

> One heavy butcher's block, with legs
> A large iron skillet
> A long threaded rod, ½ inch diameter
> Two nuts

Bore a hole in the center of the skillet, and down through the butcher's block. Braze a nut on one end of the rod. Insert the rod through the pan, and into the top of the block. Push it through as far as it will go. Put the other nut on the lower end of the rod and tighten it. To complete the skillet ashtray table, saw off the excess rod, and then hammer over the threads so the nut can't come off.

That final step is important, because for the first few days the woman will try to unbolt the skillet to take it out in the kitchen and wash it. However, if the skillet is fastened solidly and the butcher's block is heavy enough, she'll eventually give up and cheerfully admit that she's lost the battle.

The permanent ashtray can't be emptied in the normal manner, of course. When it's full, the butts must

Home Improvement and Rainy-Year Projects

either be picked out by hand or taken up with a vacuum cleaner. The latter method is much easier; it's just a matter of pursuading the woman to do it.

Landscaping and Gardening

The Law of Hopeless Landscaping, sometimes known as the Law of Copeless Handscraping, is made up of three parts as follows:

1. If you plant little trees next to your house, they will grow into giant sequoias in four years, rot out the siding, and eventually fall on your roof.

2. If you plant little trees out on the lawn away from the house, they will get no taller than your knee, and you will spend the rest of your life tripping over them and mowing around them.

3. If you plant little trees at the edge of your property, they will grow to medium height and die after your neighbor saws off half the limbs.

Unless frustration is your Thing, it's best to relax and enjoy "natural" landscaping. That's leaving the property alone and seeing what grows on it. If nothing grows, you're way ahead of the game. There will be nothing to take care of.

These are the days of "anything goes" landscaping with lawns made entirely of green pebbles illuminated at night by pink bulbs concealed in hollowed-out railroad ties. This makes it easier on the nonlandscaper and nongardener. You can get away with a yard full of poison ivy as long as you have a self-assured air, a redwood deck, and a green statue of a boy with water pouring from his armpit.

The Complete Book of Pitfalls

Learn to live with what you've got, and you'll live a lot longer. Don't fall for those articles telling you how to clear a rocky area and make a nice lawn, or how to beautify a clear area by making a rock garden. If you are perceptive, you will quickly realize that both projects involve wrestling with rocks. Moving rocks around with a crowbar isn't landscaping; it's moving rocks around.

A few years ago, a New Jersey homeowner's troubles with a single rock (which can be even worse than a married rock) made headlines in all the papers. A small stone was sticking out of his lawn. Prodded by his wife, he started to dig out the stone. He kept digging deeper and deeper. The deeper he got, the bigger the stone got. As the weeks rolled on, the stone turned into a rock turned into a boulder as big as his house. There was nothing to do (neighbors unanimously rejected a suggestion to dynamite) but shovel all the dirt back, and make a little garden around the rock. And that was one summer's landscaping project.

Even if your rocks are small enough to be moved, there's still the problem of what to do with the resulting hole. Most people give careful consideration to where they will move the rocks, but they don't think about the holes until the lawn looks like the moon. Many people who start out to make a rock garden wind up with a hole garden, which isn't the same thing at all.

Taking a live-and-let-die attitude about landscaping and gardening is difficult because the Garden Expert keeps bugging you. He writes a column about what's wrong with all the stuff growing outside, and how everything will die a painful death because of your neglect. He is always whipping you to a frenzy with things like:

"Act now, before it's too late! Dry rot is creeping into the spirea mulch this very minute!"

Home Improvement and Rainy-Year Projects

Even when the snow is howling outside and you're cozily toasting marshmallows over the hot-air register, the Garden Expert doesn't let up. He's busy warning that unless you get outside and cut back the new dead growth, the old growth will die before it gets new.

"Now's the time to prune back the roots of the Japanese Yew at least eight and a quarter inches, before the insidious Snow Fungus Canker reaches the imago stage."

In summer the Garden Expert keeps you posted on what all the insects are doing, as if anybody in his right mind would be interested in reading about flies, mosquitoes, roaches, ants, gypsy moths, gnats, waterbugs, silverfish, spiders, wasps, centipedes, bedbugs, sawtooth beetles, fleas, crickets, aphids, caterpillars, thrips, leafhoppers, cutworms, Japanese beetles, and sow bugs.

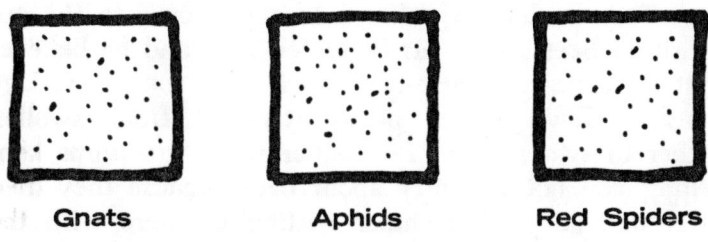

Gnats   **Aphids**   **Red Spiders**

They're all out there, eating chewing belching. "Before the first tender buds of the Climbing Mrs. VanSmythe Rose open, the rapacious Climbing Mrs. VanSmythe Mite is at work, sucking out the life-giving juices within the helpless stem.

"Look for brown spots slightly smaller than the point of a pin on the underside of the leaf, just before dawn."

The Garden Expert can't bear the sight of sap, and he goes out of his mind over winter plant damage. In spring, he advises you to venture forth, bravely, into the shrubbery to look for poor helpless twigs that have been snapped, crackled, and popped by cruel Mr. Jack Frost. You find yourself kneeling beside a plant wrapping a little white bandage around a poor twiggie wiggie, while the rest of the family stands wringing their hands.

You know from experience that the surgery is useless. Tomorrow the Garden Expert will do a whole column on the gluttonous Broken Twig Thrip.

Evidently there are no all-purpose sprays. The Garden Expert recommends something different for each bush, tree, flower, and leaf on the lawn. A powerful solution guaranteed to strangle a leaf-hopper on sight is welcomed by aphids who breathe in the heady aroma, beat their tiny chests, and return to the foliage with renewed appetites.

(Under no circumstances should you kill or injure a bee. The Garden Expert will turn you over to the authorities. Bees are on his Protected List, and he believes that old leave-bees-alone-and-they'll-leave-you alone adage handed down stings notwithstanding from swollen father to swollen son. Remember when grownups kept telling you not to worry about bees because they died after one sting? Remember getting nowhere with the childish argument that you wanted the bee to die *before* it stung you, not after? Anyway, bees are garden good guys; if you want pollination you've got to put up with pain.)

Because of today's stepped-up war against pesticides, backed by the powerful Bug Lobby, it is impossible to follow the Garden Expert's advice on sprays, anyway. Before his column rolls off the press, the poison he recommended has been taken off the market because it's poison. Somebody found out, and ratted.

Home Improvement and Rainy-Year Projects

It is a paradox that although bugs can kill a plant, you can't. Foolish indeed is the homeowner who thinks he can get rid of a bush by cutting it off at ground level. It will "come back" almost overnight. Some plants double each time you cut them down. As any mathematician will tell you, you'll be in deep trouble in no time at all.

Vines are the worst offenders. Not only are they impossible to kill but they grow amazingly fast, stopping only momentarily to pry apart shingles and loosen bricks. Before you plant a vine, ask yourself if you really want it completely covering your house and, one morning, your car.

Large-scale landscaping projects such as removing vines from the croquet court or terrace-building normally require an earth-moving machine. Dealing with bulldozer operators is a unique experience, and a word about their habits is in order. Unlike plumbers and electricians who frequently fail to keep appointments, bulldozer operators never come when they say they will. The average bulldozer operator spends 110 per cent of his time someplace else. After he fails to show up as promised, he'll give you a convincing alibi, set a firm new date, and not show up again.

His three principal excuses are:

"My machine broke down." (His machine was repossessed. He never owned a machine. He is thinking about learning how to operate a machine one of these days, and then perhaps buying or renting a machine, sometime.)

"I'm tied up with a street job." (They won't let him out of town until the cave-ins stop.)

"It's been the weather." (The weather has been too nice to operate a bulldozer.)

The Complete Book of Pitfalls

Exasperated homeowners would give anything for some inkling of the bulldozer man's timetable. The following guide may help in coordinating your landscaping project:

"I'll be over tomorrow." (Maybe next fall.)
"Saturday." (Some Saturday, some year.)
"Two weeks for sure." (Two years. For sure.)
"As soon as I finish this job." (As soon as the incumbents are thrown out of office perhaps eight or twelve years from now. His councilman brother-in-law has just landed him the municipal sewer building and sanitary landfill contracts.)
"Not till next fall." (Never.)

There is only one sure way of getting a bulldozer. Take your entire family on a European vacation. Your local excavating contractor will instantly pull his largest machine off another job, put his myopic teen-ager at the controls, and point him in the direction of your property.

When you return home, you'll be amazed at the change. And when it comes to landscaping and gardening, there's nothing like a clean start.

While-You're-at-It Projects

The man deeply involved in Home Improvement frequently finds himself working all day on a certain job but never actually starting it. Wives don't see how that's possible, and they get annoyed. They fail to appreciate the effort involved in not getting something done. They just don't understand While-You're-at-It projects.

Take the following typical situation. You've promised to saw up the tree that broke your wife's clothesline

Home Improvement and Rainy-Year Projects

when it fell over on her flower bed. You've set Saturday aside for the job. Here's what happens:

Right after breakfast, bright and early, you go out to get the big limb saw. On the way to the garage you trip over the loose porch step. You wiggle it back in place.

When you try to get into the garage to look for the saw, you have trouble lifting the overhead door. It sticks badly. The tracks and pulleys need oil. Unless the door gets immediate attention it will stick even worse, and your wife might hurt her back. You look around for the oilcan, and remember that it's in the cellar.

You go back to the house, go down to the cellar, fetch the oilcan, come back out, and trip over the other loose porch step. You put down the oilcan and examine the steps closely. The boards are rotten. They've got to be replaced. There's no time like the present, before your wife falls and hurts herself.

Building new steps requires wood, but you don't waste time looking around for scrap pieces. Every handyman knows that the quickest way to get wood for a project is to take apart something he has built.

You decide to dismantle garage shelves that really aren't being used for anything except to store empty paint cans and three-way lightbulbs two-thirds burnt out. You go up to the attic, bring down empty cardboard cartons, clear the shelves, and then take the cartons of bulbs and cans back up to the attic. You get a crowbar and hammer from the cellar, and take apart the garage shelves. You move the boards out by the porch. After finding the ruler, small hand saw, square, a pencil, and the right size nails in the cellar you start on the porch step project.

When you finish, it's time for lunch. Your wife asks

The Complete Book of Pitfalls

how the tree-sawing is going, and you say you're getting there.

After lunch you go out to get the big limb saw, trip over the oilcan on the porch, and remember that you must oil the overhead garage door. You oil the tracks but you can't reach the pulleys without a ladder. You get the stepladder from the cellar, but it won't open until you oil the hinges. After oiling the hinges and repairing a loose step, you set up the ladder, climb it, and oil the door pulleys. When you finish, you fold up the ladder and take it back to the cellar because if you don't put things away in their right places you have trouble finding them again.

You go back out to the garage and roll the door up and down a few dozen times to get it working smoothly. Then you start looking for the limb saw. You find it behind your collection of bald tires.

The saw is so rusty that you decide to oil it. But you can't find the oilcan, even in the cellar. You finally spot it on an overhead garage beam where you left it after oiling the pulleys. You can't reach it, so you go in the house to get a kitchen chair to stand on. It's easier than getting the stepladder out of the cellar again. While you're reaching up and getting the oilcan the chair wobbles. Close examination reveals the trouble—two legs and three rungs are loose.

You go down to the cellar and find the wood glue. But you can't get the cap off. You must use the workbench vise and pliers to get it unstuck. The vise almost falls off the workbench on your foot again. For several years you've been meaning to bolt it down, before it falls on one of the kids.

You have to find three $5/16$-inch bolts at least three

Home Improvement and Rainy-Year Projects

inches long, and the right nuts and washers and lockwashers. This means pawing through lots of coffee cans. Then you find the drill and proper bit, bore three holes in the workbench, and bolt down the vise.

You take the wood glue out to the garage and glue the chair rungs and legs. You fashion glue clamps out of turnbuckles from the cellar and short lengths of rope from the attic.

Excess glue squeezed from the joints must be wiped up, so you go in the house to get some rags from the bottom of the kitchen closet. While you're crouched inside the closet with a flashlight your wife asks how the tree-sawing is coming along. You tell her you're getting to it just as fast as you can.

You clean off the chair in the garage with the rags, and bring the chair inside where it's warm. After a cup of coffee, you go outside to oil the big limb saw.

It's getting dark.

There's not much point starting on the tree, since you'll have to quit right away. So you carefully oil the saw and put it back behind the bald tires. Then you gather up all the tools and take them back down to the cellar. You also take the oilcan, and while you're down there you oil some tools that show signs of rust. You also fill the oil caps on the furnace circulator motor.

You return to the kitchen, exhausted, and tell your wife that the tree-sawing project will have to wait until the following Saturday. Tomorrow is set aside for raking leaves.

As it turns out, you don't get any leaves raked that Sunday. Here's what happens:

Right after breakfast, bright and early, you go out to get the big leaf rake . . .

Tree Houses

It's easy to build a tree house for the kids if you have the time, the patience, and $500 for nails. You'll also need an expendable tree. Driving in $500 worth of nails will kill it.

An old-fashioned tree house made from old boards, with a slanted floor for water runoff, is a delight. It will be a conversation piece with neighbors, and it will devaluate your property and reduce your taxes.

Under no circumstances should you build a nice-looking structure with proper angles. Nor should it be painted. Don't get fancy. A beautiful tree house will attract the tax assessor's attention, and you'll find yourself paying taxes on an Elevated Recreation Module.

The first step is to make the ladder, and the first step in making the ladder is to make the first step. Start at the bottom, and begin nailing rungs up the tree. Two-trunk trees are better for ladders because you can fasten rungs at each end. With a single-trunk tree, you've got to nail the rungs in the middle, and they tend to swivel when you put weight on one end. If you see a squirrel hugging the trunk and gingerly testing a rung with one foot, the ladder is probably not safe for kids.

At a certain height, you'll get bored with nailing rungs, or you'll run out of rung material, or you'll get airsick. That's the point you'll start on the platform. Each tree is different (over the years you may have noticed that), but the general idea is to secure a frame to the trunk and branches. You may wish to add braces. Some tree house builders buy new framing and bracing material as a safety measure. Later you nail the rotten flooring to the good frame.

Lumberyard people are long-suffering; do-it-yourselfers are always asking for "some wood and some medium-size nails" or saying they want shingles for a roof when they mean a martin-house roof, a difference of just about two thousand shingles. Give the lumberyard folks a break and don't tell them you want framing for a house. Ask for several two-by-fours or two-by-sixes for a tree house. The length will depend on your car; if a board sticks out the window too far it hits people and fences and things. You can tell by looking at a man's tree house what size car he owns. Foreign car buffs build narrow tree houses, two or three stories high.

A man can spend all summer in a tree, sawing and hammering and yelling at the children to stay away until it's finished. Wives get used to telling people on the telephone that "he's up in the tree."

When you finally finish the tree house to your satisfaction, you'll discover it's very pleasant up there just sitting and looking around and thinking about this and that.

One of these days, though, you've got to let the kids up.

Housebuilding Don'ts

You'd be surprised at the number of inexperienced people who build houses with their own hands, and you'd be surprised at how badly these houses turn out—mainly because the builders ignored plans and planning. Housebuilding takes more than raw courage. You can't just start anywhere—say with the hall closet—and add lumber until the house is finished.

If you want to tackle a home-construction job, more power to you. But learn some basic rules first. For instance, a supporting beam must itself be supported by something. Draw accurate plans. Have an expert examine them, inch by inch. If you buy a set of house plans, go over them with the expert, and make sure you understand them.

And don't try to cut corners to save money, substituting a two-by-three where the plans call for a two-by-twelve. If the building inspector spots it, you're lucky. Otherwise you may wake up one morning with a sunken living room.

At this very moment, a house is being put together somewhere in the United States by an amateur who is convinced that any man can make his own castle as long as he has the ability to measure incorrectly, skimp on materials, dash off a nonscale drawing, and hire underage helpers at sweatshop wages to saw boards too short.

If this fellow had to live in his own house for the rest of his life, he'd get the troubles he deserved and deserve the troubles he got. But it rarely happens. After going through his first winter of indoor motion sickness, he sells the house to an unsuspecting couple who don't realize that the nice trim hides a faulty frame. The ad said, "Owner leaving town." Now they know why.

A few examples of amateur homebuilding blunders will illustrate the seriousness of the situation. All of the following are true. But you needn't worry, they don't involve the house you just bought.

Or do they?

Item—The do-it-yourselfer designed his house as he

Home Improvement and Rainy-Year Projects

Leaning Chimney

went along, drawing "plans" with a thick felt pen on shirt cardboards. When he got near the edge of a cardboard and started running out of drawing space, he made the rest of the sketch narrower to fit. Later, he had to order specially made narrow doors and windows.

Item—Several overhead light fixtures were installed near doors. When the doors swung open they just cleared the fixtures. Then the owner screwed in light bulbs, and guess what happened?

Item—After floor joists were fastened in place, the builder remembered that he hadn't left an opening for cellar stairs. Instead of cutting through one beam and boxing in the opening, he directed his gradeschool lackeys to saw crossways through eight 2 by 10 beams, removing a section from each. Those unfamiliar with construction techniques may not realize what's wrong with that procedure, and he didn't either until his floor became dish-shaped. You can't lose a marble in that house. Drop one anywhere and it will roll to a central collection point.

The Complete Book of Pitfalls

Item—A man wired his entire house with thin lamp cord. The local electrician won't even drive by the house, for fear somebody will remember his truck when the house burns down.

Item—From somewhere, an amateur builder got hold of hundreds of short boards to use as roofers. The pieces never spanned more than two rafters. Many were attached to only one. The little boards butted together over empty space. The builder learned not to step on the joints. He had an awful time nailing asphalt shingles on because the boards kept see-sawing. Now the roof leaks badly, and the owner wonders why. It's probably an exaggeration, but neighbors swear that larger birds like robins won't sit on the roof.

Item—One man built a dormer window into his master bedroom, but no closet. He neatly solved the problem by adding a door and making a closet out of the dormer alcove. Now clothes get plenty of sunlight; people get none.

Item—A professional mason was hired to build an outside chimney on a do-it-yourself house. As he laid up blocks by plumb line, he kept getting farther and farther from the wall. Perplexed, the mason climbed down his scaffold (which was built better than any part of the house), fetched a long level, and held it against the wall. The whole house was leaning. The mason asked the owner if he wanted the chimney to lean in with the house, or go straight up which would put it two feet away at the roof line. The owner said follow the house.

But don't worry, your house wasn't built by that particular incompetent. After all, your house doesn't lean.

Or does it?

IV

TIMELY TIPS FOR TIPPLY TIMES

Bee Prepared

On the surface, it would appear that the following section is a catch-all for stuff that doesn't fit anyplace else in this book. Under the surface it looks that way, too. So what's wrong with catch-alls? To survive nowadays, modern man must know a thousand and one little things, and in no particular order.

This section will cover various vital matters which otherwise might not be included for lack of a pigeonhole to put them in. Or, in which to put them, if you're a stuffy purist.

For instance, in what category would you place the warning not to drink beer or cola directly from the can, out on your patio, in summertime? When you're not looking, a bee enters the can. Then when you drink from the can, the bee stings you in the mouth. Aren't you glad to know that? Would you expect to find that under "Painting"? "Appliances"?

Then there's the kind of general advice that covers a broad field. Like you should never tell a repairman "there's no hurry." He will do absolutely nothing unless you can convince him there's an emergency. If you leave a TV set to be repaired and tell the man no hurry, he won't even glance at it. He's busy fixing sets owned by people who have threatened his life. And anybody silly enough to tell a plumber there's no hurry deserves what he gets—no plumber.

· *The Complete Book of Pitfalls*

The following pages cover everything from tips on inside jobs to hints on surviving in the grim outdoors. Pay attention, and remember, no cans on the patio.

What's the Point?

Some home building projects defeat themselves. Before you start off like a ball of fire, take a hard look at the results you expect. Often the practical advantage of all your work will be zero.

For example, building a bin out of scrap lumber to store scrap lumber won't work. When you're finished there won't be any scrap lumber to store, because you've used all of it to build the scrap lumber storage bin.

The same thing goes for overhead pipe-storage racks in the cellar, made out of the pipe you were going to put there.

People with a limited amount of living space, particularly apartment dwellers, are exhorted to build things in closets. Plans abound for closet fold-out workbenches, closet darkrooms, closet sewing centers, etc. But one practical point is never raised in the Space Saving Tips columns. Where are you supposed to put the clothes that were in the closet? There are never enough closets. Removing one is like converting your toilet bowl to a planter. Before long, you'll regret it.

Collecting Coat Hangers

If you put all your closet hangers in the same way, with the hook opening toward the back wall, all your clothes can be grabbed out easily in case of fire. Even if you're not planning to have a fire, one-way clothes hanging is a

Timely Tips for Tipply Times

good practice because you don't get that terrible tangle of wire hangers. You can easily remove the extra ones that build up and—brace yourself—THROW THEM AWAY! Such a suggestion borders on the unspeakable, since everybody in the United States collects coat hangers. The more valuable specimens are displayed on the rod in close formation; the thousand or so remaining hangers repose on the closet shelf and on the floor with the old shoe collection.

It takes courage to throw away a "good" coat hanger, but this year you really must try.

Pigs at Speed

Store children's records in a separate place, otherwise your guests will be startled out of their wits when the soft classical music is suddenly interrupted by "I'm a gingerbread boy, I am; I can run from you!" or the piercing ocarina refrain from "Rapunzel."

While you're going through your records, use an indelible marker to write clearly on each children's record the speed it should be played. Children have four speeds to choose from these days—16, 33⅓, 45, 78—and they invariably select the wrong one. This is hard on grown-ups. When a 45 rpm "Three Little Pigs" record is played at 33⅓, the pigs sound more like the three bears with too many Manhattans under their belts, kind of slow and slurred. The same record played at 16 sounds like they've been drinking since breakfast. Much of what the bears (really pigs) say comes out "Wrrowrarrrrrrr" in the low low registers. If the lever is pushed up to 78, the pigs sound like a convention of mice, and a limp-wristed Big Bad Wolf is extremely annoying.

Down with Wattage

Men, one way to lower your light bill is to gradually replace all the bulbs in the house with ones of lower wattage. Wait a while, then substitute still smaller bulbs. Done sneakily over a long period of time, a 150-watt bulb in the laundry can be brought down to a glowing 15 watts without your wife noticing it. At 7½ watts, she'll probably complain that it seems kind of dim in here. Show immediate solicitude by putting the 15-watter back in. Tell her you've made it twice as bright.

Storing Small Parts

Despite what they say in electronics magazines, it's not a good idea to store small parts in muffin tins. Wives retaliate by storing muffins in small parts bins. An egg carton works just as well, unless an egg has leaked in one of the compartments. Then it takes three weeks to get all the gooey egg off the tiny watch gear.

When taking apart an appliance, the parts can be placed on a sticky-side-up strip of masking tape fastened to the table. The parts will stay neatly in the right order, until your sleeve touches the tape.

Screwing Up a Chair

If a wood screw in an old chair works loose and won't grip, remove the screw, put match sticks in the hole, break them off flush, and re-drive the screw. This old home-repairman's trick will keep the chair from wob-

Timely Tips for Tipply Times

bling for several months. Then what you do is remove the screw, put more match sticks in the hole, break them off flush, and re-drive the screw. In ten years, the chair will be made entirely of match sticks.

Fetching Wrong Wrenches

Before you start working on nuts and bolts make sure all your wrenches are at the job site. Otherwise you'll make the same mistake people make all their lives with wrenches. First you'll glance at the nut to be loosened, and then you'll try to fetch the correct wrench from the house. It will be the wrong size every time, usually too small. Then you'll go back to the house and get a larger wrench. It will still be too small. This will go on and on until you finally bring out a wrench that is slightly too large for the nut. If you use that one, it will keep slipping, smoothing off the corners until you have a round nut you can't grip with any size wrench.

Don't even attempt to work on American nuts with British metric-scale wrenches. They're *all* the wrong size.

No matter how easy it looks, only a skilled mechanic can look at a nut and tell what size wrench will fit it. You can easily wear out a pair of strong work shoes in a single day, just walking back and forth with wrong-sized wrenches.

Totem Poles at Home

Don't throw away old wooden window shade rollers. Cut away the hollow part where the spring was, and use the rest of the roller for carving miniature totem poles. The softwood rollers are excellent for this purpose. All things considered, window shade rollers make better totem poles than window shade rollers.

Nailing Boards

If you drive a nail near the end of a board, the board will often split. When nailing boards together, drill a pilot hole first, and the top board won't split. The other board will split.

Dividing Boards

A board may be divided into equal parts, long-way, by slanting a ruler across the board at the desired number of divisions. Mark the divisions, and then do the same thing at the other end of the board. Carefully join the marks with a fine pencil along a straightedge. Then whack the board with an ax.

Fastening Things to Walls

A simple magnetic device helps you find the vertical wooden studs behind the wallboard in newer buildings. The stud-finder's magnetic needle is attracted to the plastered-over nails in the studs. You mark the location of each nail lightly with a pencil. A line drawn through all the marks shows where the stud is. When hanging heavy shelves, pictures, or moose heads, the hangers must be fastened securely into the studs. Don't hang heavy objects on the weak wallboard unless you like the sound of things crashing in the middle of the night.

Timely Tips for Tipply Times

For light pictures and decorations, hollow wall fasteners with expanding ribs or wings are available. You drill a hole in the wall, insert the device, and if you've followed directions it will anchor itself to the wall. If you haven't followed directions it will go all the way through the hole and drop down inside. Then you can wring your hands and start all over again.

For extremely lightweight applications, there are hangers that just stick to the wall surface. These are risky, because they're only as strong as the surface coating. If the paint or wallpaper is peeling, you can expect the sticker hanger to peel off with it.

When in doubt, anchor a picture hook directly to the wooden framing. The studs are hard to find in older houses; sometimes there appear to be none at all. It often seems that old-time carpenters deliberately set out to hide the studs. Framing is haphazard. If your stud-finder detects a beam near the floor, there is no guarantee it will still be behind the wall at picture-hanging level. Somewhere in between, it has wandered off someplace.

The only time studs are plentiful is when an old house is being wrecked. Removing the walls reveals trillions of studs crisscrossing everywhere and only inches apart. The wreckers have to use dynamite to break up the frame. And yet strangely enough, several generations of people living in that house could never find a place to put a picture nail.

Opening Other Garages

Electronic garage door openers are a nice luxury as long as everybody on the block isn't on the same frequency. Before installing one, check around to see what other

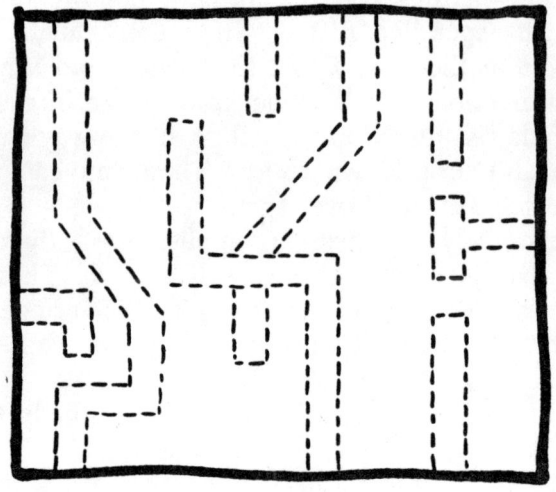

Studs Behind Walls

doors your transmitter will control. You won't have a peaceful neighborhood if garage doors rumble up and down all night every time anybody pushes a button.

Parking Tip

Some people have trouble positioning a car in a garage. You can get it right every time if you hang a string from the ceiling with a small weight such as a washer tied to it. The washer should just hit the windshield in front of the driver when the car is in place. It is easy to see, and after a while you'll be able to whip in the garage and park perfectly every time.

Timely Tips for Tipply Times

Parking Trick

A wonderful practical joke to play on a fellow who has a car-positioning string hanging from his garage ceiling is to sneak in while he's away and move the string two feet toward the back wall.

Bashing a Porch

A porch that has been knocked out of line by a car, or a flood, or a kid running from hornets can be set back in place again with two tools—a car jack and a sledgehammer. Jack up a corner of the porch and hit it with the sledge until it moves a bit and falls off the jack. Repeat the performance until the porch is back in place and you've attracted spectators from all over the neighborhood.

Water and Oil

Make sure outside fuel oil fill-caps are screwed on tightly. Little children like to play Oil Delivery Man. All they need is a garden hose.

Wearing Out from No Wear

Oil burner emergency switches sometimes go bad and require replacement. They're the ones with the red switchplate, usually found near the cellar door. Experts insist that the reason these switches go bad is because they're hardly ever used. In other words, the less wear a switch gets the quicker it wears out. That's difficult to believe, but so are a lot of things.

One Leg Out

The straight-faced statement by an electrician that "You've got one leg out" often leads to misunderstanding. One of the most peculiar expressions of the trade, it means that one portion, or "leg" of a 230-volt, three-wire circuit isn't working. After a lightning storm when your stove only gets warm or when half of the lights won't work, chances are you've got one leg out. Don't get indignant about it; relax and be thankful you don't have both legs out.

Heating Up Birds

An expensive way to attract birds in winter is to install a clothes dryer in the basement with an outlet pipe through the window. Birds like to stand in the pipe's blast of hot air, fluffing their feathers. If you put out food, many birds will hang around the pipe all winter, picking their teeth and telling dirty stories instead of flying south.

Choking Roses

Don't leave those little wire tags on rose bushes. As the plant grows, the wire will begin to choke the stem. Nobody likes the sound of gagging in the garden. If you

Timely Tips for Tipply Times

want to remember names and locations, position hooks on a board and hang the tags on them.

Space-saver

Space between walls, the depth of the 2 by 4 studs, can be utilized for built-in medicine cabinets, fishing rod racks, fold-down ironing boards, knickknack shelves, etc. Don't use exterior walls in cold climates, though. You'd have to remove insulation, and your medicines and knickknacks would freeze.

Leave Folding Chairs Alone

Children like to wrestle with folding chairs. Let them. Don't attempt to open a folding chair when there's a kid around. Kids like to rescue helpless grownups. If he pinches his finger on the chair, so much the better. He's learning about Life.

Install Valves

All hot and cold water lines leading to faucets should have shut-off valves. Not only do they save a lot of running around looking for the master valve when a pipe springs a leak, but you can change a faucet washer without shutting down the entire system.

Funny-sounding Pipes

When pipes make funny noises, there are several things you can do. Moving away is one of them. While that

The Complete Book of Pitfalls

makes a lot of sense, you may for one reason or another prefer to stay and fight the pipes. Try wedging pieces of cardboard or small sticks between the pipe and the overhead beam; it often stops vibration. The same trick works with pipes "buzzing" against a wall.

If you get "air hammer" when you close a faucet, you can install an antihammer air chamber in the water line. The easiest way to prevent "air hammer," however, is to avoid turning on the water in the first place. This also saves water.

Sometimes you'll hear a chattering noise. That usually signifies a bad faucet washer, or a red squirrel.

Point to Ponder

Paint stores give you a free yardstick to measure lumber. Lumber yards give you a free paint-stirring stick. You figure it out.

Shady Painting

In hot weather, avoid painting in direct sunlight. The sun dries the paint too fast for it to "stick" properly. Also, you may get heat exhaustion and fall off the ladder. Paint the shady side of the house until the sun strikes it; then move around in the shade again. Follow this procedure every day. Eventually you'll have the best painted house in the neighborhood, and the poorest suntan.

Timely Tips for Tipply Times

Unlevel Levels

Discount stores actually sell carpenter's levels stamped "Second." The levels look all right; it's just that they're not level. Don't buy an unlevel level. It's not good for much of anything except pounding stakes. (See section on Tools.)

Another discount store eyebrow-raiser—a display of car compasses all pointing in a different direction. The only thing more useless than an unreliable compass or an unlevel level is a carton of last year's calendars.

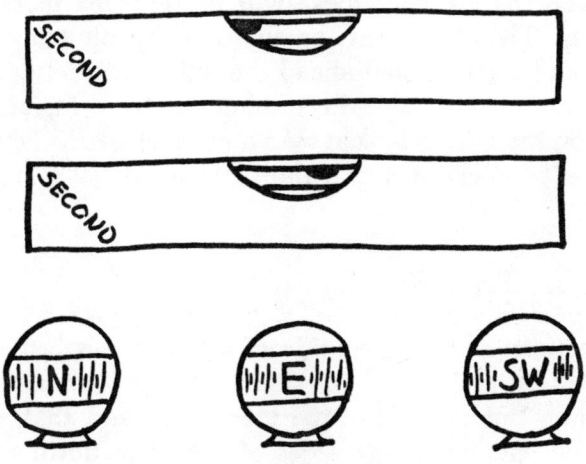

Puzzling Store Displays

Dogs Know These Things

A dog knows when you're building him a doghouse. You must keep a dog away from the site because he'll interfere with the work. He gets excited, chews the boards and tools, gets in the way of the saw, and tries to move in before you've finished. Never attempt to build a doghouse with a dog helping you.

Time Tip

To set electric clocks back an hour just pull the plugs, wait an hour, and plug them back in again. Use a wind-up clock to tell when the hour is up. Remembering to look at the wind-up clock is the tricky part. If you forget, then the electric clocks will be set back more than an hour. Then you must compensate by plugging them all in, and setting them ahead the difference between the time they should have been plugged back in, and the time you thought to look at the wind-up clock.

Some people just shove the little hand back an hour.

The Tree Race

Tree experts say the east side of a tree grows faster than the west side. They claim that morning light is 20 per cent more intense than afternoon light, and that, therefore, the east and south sides of a tree in northern latitudes grow better than the west and north sides.

The solution to the problem is to prune a little more in the east and south to keep the tree symmetrical, say the experts.

Now that you know about trees growing unevenly, you'll no longer look at one with serene thoughts. Think of the tree struggling with itself, day after day. If you

Timely Tips for Tipply Times

listen carefully, you can hear creaking and groaning. It's the west and north sides, losing.

Instant Bad Furniture

You can make a bookcase out of used boards and old bricks. It looks terrible.

Have an Ornament Shoot

Trimming a Christmas tree is a delight; untrimming it is a chore. This Christmas, why not stage an ornament shoot? You take the whole tree outdoors and shoot off the ornaments with a BB gun. Charge admission per shot, and let the whole neighborhood relieve holiday tensions by blazing away at the tree.

If you figure the fees right, you'll get enough to pay for a new set of ornaments next year. But best of all, you won't have to untrim your tree.

The Sporting Life

Sporting-goods stores now offer a device that throws beer cans in the air for target practice. Powered by .22 blanks, it has a range of forty yards. It is excellent for lobbing empties over the neighbor's fence.

Look-alike Hazards

To insure domestic tranquillity, they should stop making the following things that look alike and are mistaken for one another:

The Complete Book of Pitfalls

1. Car windshield de-icer and artificial snow for holiday decorations. Both come in the same size spray cans, with a picture of Jack Frost. De-icer sprayed on furniture removes the finish, and "snow" sprayed on the windshield removes the car-owner's cool.
2. Grated Parmesan cheese and scouring powder. Each is packed in a cylindrical container with holes in the top. Each has white lettering on a background of red, yellow, and a particular shade of electric green. The cleanser tastes terrible on spaghetti, and the cheese gums up the sink.
3. Clear quart bottles of quinine water and club soda. In this case the labels are of different colors, but the beverages inside look exactly alike. When both bottles are handy at a party, a Scotch drinker will always get Scotch and quinine water, no matter what the law of averages says.
4. Spout cans of household oil and of lighter fluid. Anybody who keeps them in the same closet on the same shelf eventually will fill his lighter with household oil. Then the lighter won't light unless the wick is ignited with a match. It burns like a smudge-pot. It's a fine opportunity to quit smoking, or to start growing oranges.

Mattresses Resist

The most difficult thing in the world to carry is a mattress. It resists by going limp, like a demonstrator. If two people try to carry it, the middle folds. If you lean it against the wall while you catch your breath, it slowly slumps to the floor and dies.

The only way to transport a mattress is to roll it up

Timely Tips for Tipply Times

first. You'll need at least five people because a mattress doesn't like to be rolled. It fights back. After you get it rolled tight, don't make the common mistake of securing it with a couple pieces of twine. The mattress will strain against its bonds and break loose at the very moment you're carrying it past the glass cupboard. Use heavy rope to tie a mattress, and don't let it out of your sight for a second.

How to Be Quoted

The principal advantage to living in the city is that you're where the action is. The principal advantage to living in the suburbs is that you have some air to breathe.

The principal advantage to living in the country is that city people stop to ask directions, giving you the opportunity to say something witty which will be printed in *Reader's Digest*.

When you first move to your country home, make careful preparations for direction-giving. Rehearse replies, like "There ain't no way to get there from here, Bub; you gotta start someplace else."

Or: "Road's a mite rough; it's ten miles, and the crows walk."

Dress for the occasion—tattered mackinaw in winter, bib "overhauls" in summer. Spend as much time as you can puttering around near the road. Practice spitting before you speak. Squint at the sun a lot. Learn how to scratch thoughtfully.

Finally the big day will arrive. Rich city folk will stop and ask if they're on the right road to Moodyville. Straighten up slowly, spit to one side, and amble toward

The Complete Book of Pitfalls

their big car. The occupants will get out pencils in preparation for "$200 for Life in These United States."

If you can't think of anything to say immediately, that's okay. They'll mistake silence for wisdom. But eventually you'll have to make some remark, if only an obscure one like, "Colder it gets, easier wood splits."

If you tell them they're on the right road and let it go at that you've failed as a Roadside Sage, of course. You might as well move back to the city.

"Handyman's Special"

Beware of a house advertised in the paper as a "Handyman's Special." That house is owned by the same fellow who's trying to sell a car that "Needs some body work." It rolled off a cliff.

The ad says that the Handyman's Special house "has lots of potential" and just needs "a little fixing up by somebody who likes to putter around with tools." In advertising lingo, that means the house must be torn down to ground level and rebuilt providing the foundation is good and that's hard to tell about because you can't inspect it, the cellar being full of water and all.

Flood-It-Yourself

Flooded basements were once a problem of great concern to homeowners. But that was before the Civil Defense organization pointed out that a flooded basement can be a good thing, and that on special occasions a homeowner should consider flooding his own basement.

Timely Tips for Tipply Times

In a pamphlet titled "In Time of Emergency," the Office of Civil Defense devotes a chapter to floods and hurricanes, and advises:

> In most cases, it is better to permit the flood waters to flow freely into the basement. Or flood the basement yourself with clean water, if you feel sure it will be flooded anyway. This will equalize the water pressure on the inside and outside of the basement walls and floor, and thus avoid structural damage to the foundation and the house.

You'll have to decide yourself, of course, when your basement "will be flooded anyway." Then you've got to convince your wife that it's a good idea to open the taps and cover the furnace and the washer and the dryer and the stored clothes and everything else down there with water. At this point, you'll have to take steps to avoid personal structural damage. If you can survive, you should have no trouble with floods and hurricanes.

Relocation Guidelines

When looking for a new place to live, there are many important things to consider. You must first ask yourself what you really want in a house or apartment. Even before that, you should ask yourself if you want a house or an apartment. Or do you want to live in a trailer? Or a cave? Houseboat? Castle? After you've asked yourself these questions, answer them. But try not to get involved in a loud argument. And watch your language.

Perhaps it would be better to seek outside help. What

do others look for? What are the "musts"? Naturally, since individual needs and tastes differ, it is difficult to set forth a firm set of relocation rules. But there are guidelines. Veteran real estate men say that prospective buyers and renters usually insist on one or more of the following desirable features:

1. A house on a hill in the woods with a view, with a trout stream running up one side of the hill, past the house, and down the other side.

2. A community with strict laws against air pollution and noise, but with plenty of heavy industry to ease the tax burden.

3. An apartment with only one entrance to make it more burglar-proof, but with several exits in case of fire.

4. A desert hacienda, close to shops.

5. A rustic hideaway with very low property taxes, but with basic essential services such as a new school with the best teachers, underground telephone and power lines, street lights and sidewalks, gas lines, municipal sewer and water service, and a nearby freeway with no traffic.

6. Plenty of police and fire protection, with departments staffed by dedicated career men willing to take risks and serve a grateful community which pays them $6,500 a year tops.

7. A long, winding, private lane, maintained by the Road Department.

8. Three or four air-conditioned rooms in a two-story brick building, each building having its own courtyard and lawn area, with garage and laundry facilities at sub-surface level. But not garden apartments.

9. A tight, draft-free villa with a working fireplace in each room, easy to keep clean.

Timely Tips for Tipply Times

10. A ground-floor penthouse.

11. A nearby railroad that encourages passengers, runs on time, and has not filed a bankruptcy petition.

12. A hot, dry climate, cooled with an ocean breeze.

13. A charming, two-century-old stone house with everything new and modern inside and out.

14. A mountaintop chalet, out of the wind and weather.

15. A new ranch-style or colonial-style house on a newly cleared tract with a little ground around it, but with a sufficient number of neighbors in the same income bracket so you'll have something in common, and so the kids will have somebody to play with. And new streets, and perhaps a nice community recreation area. But not in a development, God forbid.